ROCKERS

AND

ROLLERS

ROCKERS AND ROLLERS

A FULL-THROTTLE MEMOIR

BRIAN JOHNSON

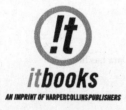

itbooks

AN IMPRINT OF HARPERCOLLINS PUBLISHERS

*it*books

A version of this book was published in 2009 in the U.K. by Michael Joseph, an imprint of the Penguin Group, Penguin Books Ltd.

A hardcover edition of this book was published in 2011 by It Books, an imprint of HarperCollins Publishers.

HarperCollins books may be purchased for educational, business, or sales promotional use. For information please write: Special Markets Department at SPsales@harpercollins.com.

First It Books paperback published 2012.

Library of Congress Cataloging-in-Publication Data has been applied for.

ISBN 978-0-06-199084-7

HB 12.16.2022

Contents

ROCKERS
AND
ROLLERS

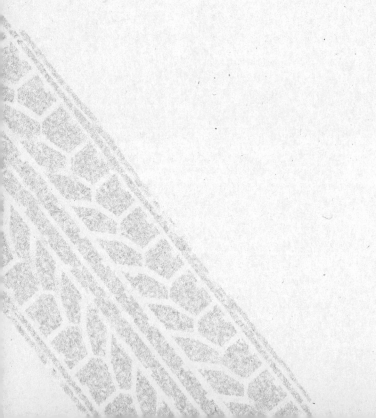

The Last Chapter

REFLECTING ON THE END OF THE BEGINNING

As I finish writing this exercise in fun and self-indulgence, I can only think that we, the generations of people from the 1920s till now and probably the next thirty years, we are the ones who drove cars, real cars. We are the ones who rode in the steam and diesel trains; some of us were lucky enough to fly in Concorde, to listen to the growl of a V8 Chevy engine, the purr of a Ferrari. We are the ones who could watch cars and motorcycles racing against each other and not feel like criminals. We are the ones who could still get speeding tickets, impress girls with our cars first and penis engineering afterwards.

Someone picking this up in 2050 might be being transported in God knows what, some grass-powered hybrid. We have been the lucky generations. And that's why every new car, every turn of the ignition key, is a new baby to me. It's what man's made out of nature. It's rock 'n' roll.

Do I like cars?!

Kids in Dunston

EXPLORING DANGEROUS PLACES

When we were kids in Dunston, a former mining village just outside Newcastle on the banks of the River Tyne, there were places we were told not to go. And, of course, that's where we went—basically, anywhere dangerous. The power station was definitely off-limits, because of the slag heaps, which held water and also created a form of quicksand. But in between the dangerous bits there were old army trucks and old railway carriages. The carriages, they were red and cream with wood linings inside and beautiful lamps over the tables. The seats were a red-patterned cloth with high backs and headrests. I was completely and utterly in love with both the trains and the trucks.

I would ride my bike down there and climb into the cab of one of those old army three-tonners. Oh, the smell, I could never figure out what that smell was. But I ignored it and, just like at home, with my bed steering wheel, I'd drive, but this was real—this had pedals I couldn't reach and a gearstick. My God, I was at Normandy, then North Africa, Anzio—a fearless driver getting the ammunition through to the front line. Then I'd run to the railway carriages and sit in them, yeah, just sit in them, because they were posh with a capital *P*. And there was that smell again: what the hell was that smell?

Years and years later, I still remember that smell, and I think I've figured it out. It was the smell of sadness, of things that weren't broken but had been left to rot, surplus to requirements. Ah, shit . . .

P.S.: It was also at this place, one Sunday afternoon, that about nine of us gathered, and one particular lad—who shall remain nameless—said his older brother had just shown him a new trick called wanking. He got out his tadger (for that is what we called our tadgers), and proceeded with two fingers to jerk it up and down. Oh, how we laughed. Then he said, "C'mon, everybody do it, or I'll bash you up!" He was a tough guy. We all did it, none of us had an orgasm or anything near one—how can you, when you're thinking of a three-ton Bedford army truck?

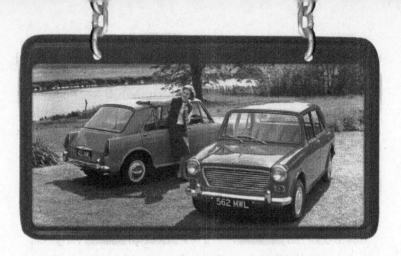

The Driving Test

THE HARROWING ADVENTURES OF THE ROAD TEST

The driving test: the final frontier, the *High Noon* of exams. I was eighteen years old, and I enrolled at the British School of Motoring to prepare for it. I was to drive in a Morris 1100, the Alec Issigonis–designed car with a sideways mounted engine with an 1100-cc (or 1.1-liter) power plant. It was powder blue, unlike my instructor's nose, which was end-of-cock purple. He had what I thought was a tiny mustache, but on closer inspection turned out to be nose hairs that looked like two hairy pussies side by side. His eyebrows were like a relief map of the Himalayas. They just went everywhere. He wore a three-quarter-length coat and a five-and-three-quarter-size trilby hat on his head. He was constantly blowing his nose and checking the contents of his handkerchief. He was as friendly as a male gorilla with nothing to shag! And lucky me had him all to myself for one whole hour.

"Get in the vehicle."

Christ, "the vehicle"—what the hell?

"You will address me as Mr. Mephistopheles at all times. You will follow my instructions and you will not deviate from them. You will not turn to face me when you are driving. You vill obey my orders at all times, and YOU VILL BE SHOT IF YOU GO OVER THIRTY MILES AN HOUR!"

Now, he didn't look German (well, not with those nose hairs). The lesson itself was a blur. All I remember is that he shouted a lot and said "No! No! No!" all the time. Basically, he was as bad at instructing as I was at driving. And I still had five more lessons.

In between lessons, I read the driver's bible—*The Highway Code*. You had to memorize every bloody thing in it, for the theory part of the test.

After my sixth lesson, "Hair Face" turned to me and said, "You've no chance of passing your test."

"Why?" I asked.

"Because you're shite."

Ah, nothing like a gentle letdown! Of course, he was right. I sat the test and failed. And yup, it was the questions that I screwed up.

Examiner: "Right, when should you never overtake?"

Me: "Erm . . . on the brow of a hill."

Examiner: "I need two more."

Me: "Erm . . . on the brow of another hill?"

He was not a humorous man and it all went downhill from there. Dejected and hurt, I sloped off home. I applied for another shot at it the next day. I suddenly realized what I had been doing wrong, twit that I was. At home, I had been practicing with a Ford Popular with its three gears and then spending only one hour a week in the more modern Morris 1100 with its four gears, so I never really got used to it. At that time, I was in my first band (The Gobi Desert Canoe Club). Our guitarist, Trevor Chance, had a four-gear Mini Minor, so I asked him if I could drive his car when we were having band practice and sit my test in it. He said yes, no problem, Brian—after I'd handed him some money.

The upshot was that I sat my test six weeks later. The examiner was a nice guy. He told me we were going to Dunston to do the test—that was my own backyard. At the end, he said, "You've passed, Mr. Johnson. Well done!" I drove straight to the pub to celebrate.

It was one of those days that your youth gobbles up, an achievement that youth deserves, and being young you drink it in like fine wine—a bit like losing your virginity. I know I'm waxing lyrical, but shit! You'd overcome machinery. You were "the man." You were flying solo. You could go anywhere you wanted, on your own—all the things I'd dreamt of as a kid (though I was still a kid, really, at eighteen). I'll bet there's not one of you out there reading this who doesn't remember that day, that feeling of freedom.

Tour Bus

NOT YOUR FATHER'S TOUR BUS STORY

A tour bus is something every groupie wants to see the roof of and every male rock fan wants to see the inside of. They are amazing vehicles; the Americans make the best ones, and they're called Prevost and are fabulously rock 'n' roll. The British and European ones are crrrap! The English build the coachwork, so it's, "Let's make really small seats and make everyone feel as uncomfortable as possible." The chassis are usually made by Volvo, Swedish by name, Swedish by nature. Dull. One big safety bollocks after another, with tremendous discomfort on top. It's one of the few times in life you wanna drive American.

The adventures on American buses are legend. Take, for instance, the time when one of our drivers was a devout born-again Christian, and we got ten gorgeous groupies to get down on all fours eating and sucking each other's thingies all the way down the bus to the driving seat, and when the front girl unzipped his pants and gave him his first blow job, his first words were "Oh, my Lord!" Other truckers passing were honking horns and calling him on his CB. All ten girls gave oral communion to our Christian friend. He never called on the Lord again, but he did maintain a steady 70 mph. What a driver!

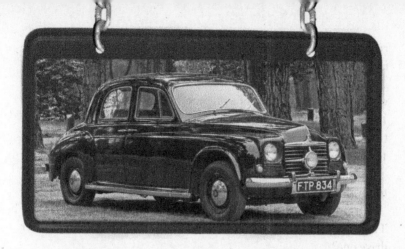

Rovers and Rollers

DEAD OR ALIVE, YOU WILL BE DRIVEN IN STYLE

I was born on October 5, 1947, in the village of Dunston-on-Tyne. The eldest of four, I was brought up in a council house, or government housing, just like all the other kids. Our dads were hardworking, hard-drinking Geordies: miners, steelworkers, shipbuilders, fitters, and turners. My dad, God bless him, worked in the foundry. What a comedown. Back from the war, where he had been a sergeant major in the Durham Light Infantry, he took the first job he could.

Like everyone else in Dunston, he couldn't afford a car. He didn't even own a motorcycle. Factory foremen drove old Ford Populars and Austins, but there wasn't much to get excited about. Until you had to call out the doctor. When I was ten, I wound up with double pneumonia. If it hadn't been for Dr. Fairbairn's reliable Rover, I wouldn't be here today, banging on to you, my fellow car nuts. There was only a fifty-fifty chance of me getting through the night.

"Pull through, son, and you can have a ride in my Rover," said Dr. Fairbairn. It was a big, posh car, a four-door saloon with chrome runners and headlights the size of my head. Staring up at the enormous grille was like staring up at the Empire State Building.

Now, if the doctor didn't make it in time—or when your time was up—you got the ride of a lifetime. Funeral cars were shiny black 1930s Rolls-Royces. Huge buggers, they were light-years ahead of the competition with their 6-cylinder, 7.7-liter engines producing 113 horsepower.

"It'll be my turn to ride in a Rolls-Royce soon," the old men used to say.

To a little boy, they were even more impressive than a Rover. They were cars fit for kings and queens. Didn't the prime minister drive one?

"Why are the doors so big?" I said to Pops as we stood on a street corner, watching a procession of them go by. "So they can get in with their top hats on," he said.

He meant it, too.

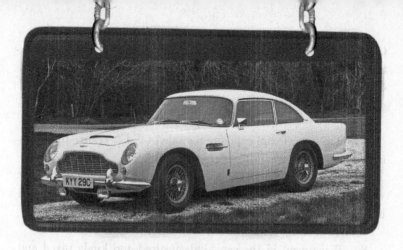

Cliff Williams

OCCUPATION: WORLD'S BEST ROCK 'N' ROLL
BASS PLAYER

In the mid-eighties, Cliff visited me in Newcastle. We had a break before playing Glasgow Apollo. Near my house, there was an upmarket used-car dealership, and as we passed it one day, Cliff shouted, "Whoa, Jonna, look at that, mate!" I did look, and there in the window was an Aston Martin DB5, dark blue, with a beautiful wide-mouthed front, looking just like a woman's vertical thingy. Red interior—what else! It was quite stunning.

"I got to have it," he said.

"But, Cliff," I said, "you live in Hawaii."

"Do I?" he said.

Oh, oh, he was gone. Car brain-freeze. He hadn't even asked how much it was, and had already written out the check. This car can do that to you. The salesman said, "Well, sir, we haven't fully checked it out, but I drove it to work this morning and it runs fine."

Oh no, he was lying without lying. Cliff had that look on his face like someone was still giving him a blow job. "Snap out of it, mate!

Come back. Don't go into the light!" I tied a rope 'round his waist, but it was too late. The salesman had opened the driver's door and Cliff was in the driving seat. His brain wasn't, and his wallet had gone bye-byes with it.

"Cliff," I said, "we're due in Glasgow in two hours, mate."

"Oh! I'm sure we can expedite the sale." I didn't realize the salesman was a sailor.

"Yes, yes," said Cliff. The saliva falling from his mouth was at washing-machine-overspill level. He stopped still, eyes thoughtful; it looked like it hurt. "I'll drive it to Glasgow."

"What!" I said. "It hasn't even been checked out."

So off we went in the car, kinda insured and kinda taxed and kinda checked over. It would have been kinda smart to leave it there. But Cliff loved the car. It smelled like Sherlock Holmes's office, all wood paneling and shiny knobs and stuff. We were on our way to Glasgow.

"Hey, Jonna, it's a noisy bugger," Cliff said.

"Try second gear, mate. We're doing sixty in first."

"Oh bugger, I'm so used to automatics in the States."

"Third and fourth's not a bad option either." His driving technique was to have dire consequences later that day. Half an hour later, Cliff said, "Hey, Jonna, it's raining, mate. Where's the wiper switch?"

"I think it's that one on the dash that says wipers."

"Oh yeah." He flicked it—nothing. A few more flicks and definitely *mort*. It was a part of the car that hadn't been fully checked out. Now, it's really pissing down and we can't see a thing. We pull over, and I remember an old trick. We take off our sneaker laces and tie them together, then 'round the wiper blade and through both windows, Cliff pulls one end and I pull the other back. It's crude, but it works, providing you're doing 30 mph.

"It's fucking working, Jonna! We're going to make it."

"Have you farted?" I asked Cliff.

"Not recently," he replied.

"Well, somebody has, unless we're passing one of those shite farms."

"Is that fog, Jonna?"

"Ah shit, Cliff, that's steam coming from under the hood, mate. Pull into the first garage you see." Well, we were on the A69 road to the M6, where garages are rarer than rocking-horse shit, so we go off the road and stop at a small village garage. We opened the hood and unleashed a cloud of steam. The mechanic pulled his head out from under the hood. "Aye, son, ya cylinder head gasket's gone."

Oh no, another bit that hadn't been fully checked. We hurriedly phoned our tour manager and told him what happened, and he hurriedly told us what a pair of idiots we were. We hired a taxi. The driver was a very happy man, driving us the eighty miles to Glasgow. When we got there, he turned around to look at us and said, "Y'know, lads, I've never been to a foreign country before."

The garage was going to trailer the Aston Martin back to the dealer in Newcastle. Cliff was pissed off. "What a piece of shit, Jonna. I can't believe I did that. I'll never buy another Aston Martin as long as I live."

Cliff now lives in Savannah, Georgia, and he drives an Aston Martin DB9.

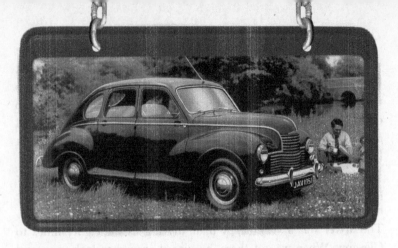

Beauty and the Beast

Here I have to introduce one of my first loves—and hates. The Jowett Javelin was a sleek, aerodynamic, metallic blue—gold, if you were lucky—exotic bird of a car. In the early fifties, British middle management fell in love with her. She had "class." Spotting one of these gorgeous cars on a dull Tyneside morning made my heart beat faster. It was a short-lived fancy. They finished manufacturing them in 1953. They were too beautiful to survive England in the fifties, if you ask me. At the other end of the spectrum was Uncle Bill's Vauxhall, a car I will forever associate with the bitter pill of disappointment. "I've got the Vauxhall out the front," he'd say. Uncle Bill was a dapper man who fancied himself as a bit of a lad. The shame of it was that he delivered bread for Hunters the Bakers. "If I can be of any assistance . . . ?" was another of his lines.

One summer, Pops decided to take him up on his offer. Uncle Bill was dispatched to drive us to a trailer, khaki, ex-army, on the top of a windy cliff in the harbor town of Amble. My father had rented it from one of his workmates, and thought he had himself a bargain.

Well, it was the closest one to the pub. If we tried to play football, the winds would send the ball into Cumbria. When we got an ice cream, the gulls would attack us. Would we make it through the week? At night, it was hard to sleep with the trailer rocking to and fro with the gales—dreams of being blown over the cliff onto the rocks below. Oh yeah, and it didn't have a heater. It was the worst holiday of my life. Pops spent his days—and nights—in the pub. Mum wept. She was from southern Italy, met her sergeant major in the war and followed him back to rainy Tyneside. It was the biggest mistake of her life. The kids fought. At the end of a week, Uncle Bill picked us up in the Vauxhall and drove us home.

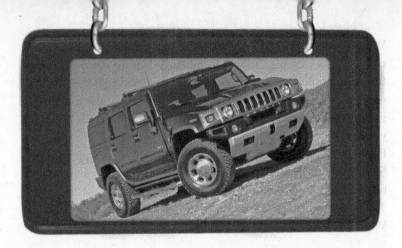

The Hummer and The Schwarzenegger

AC/DC, AN AUSTRIAN, A MUSIC VIDEO, AND A RATHER LARGE VEHICLE

I bought my Hummer 3 about six years ago. I sold my Hummer 3 about six years ago. I don't even know why I bought it. (I think it's because whenever I climbed into the cab, I thought I was Sergeant Fury. At night, when I drove to people's houses, they'd come out with their hands up, screaming, "Don't shoot!" It was that intimidating.) It was big, it was daft, and if someone shot your tires, they could reinflate themselves—brilliant! And I made firm friends at all my local filling stations: it was a thirsty bugger. But I soon realized it was nothing like the real thing. It was second-rate, like screwing a woman who's been put away damp. It was the sum of all things silly.

Now the *real* Humvee is a different animal altogether, which reminds me of a time in Van Nuys, California. AC/DC were shooting a video for the song "Big Gun," which was being used in the movie

Last Action Hero. We were having lunch outside, when a great big Humvee the color of a camel's arse flew by and nearly clipped the table. We went flying.

"You idiot!" I shouted. The Humvee stopped, and out sloped a big muscle with a head on top. Oops, he's a big bugger! It was Arnold "Schwarzenaustrohungarianegger," and he had his "Aahh'll be baaack" sunglasses on. Was that a smile or a grimace on his face? He looked like he'd just lost a dollar and found a quarter, d'ya know what I mean? He tractored towards us. I noticed his head never moved when he walked. He walked past and lifted a finger, which obviously meant, "Hey, guys, lovely to see you. This is going to be fun." You see, Arnie was going to be in the video.

Now I had to inspect the Humvee. God, it was big, as wide as a diner counter, just not as shiny. On a foggy day, you wouldn't be able to see who was sitting next to you, it was so wide. The inside was all military. There were levers and knobs everywhere. So this was Arnie's ride. Well, of course it was. He had to drive something that was him, an action-mobile.

What happened next floored me. Arnie came out of his trailer wearing an Angus schoolboy suit, complete with guitar. At first I thought someone had left an air hose up Angus's arse, but no, it was Arnie, ready to rock. And rock he did! He mimed a duet with Angus, then picked Angus up with one arm and sat him on his shoulder. You know, this guy was all right. I asked Arnie about his Humvee, and the quietest man I know started to talk about his car (it's always the way with cars). He loved it. "It fitz my sholterz," he said, and he started to heave with laughter.

But he wasn't kiddin'. I saw the label inside his leather jacket: it was XXXXL.

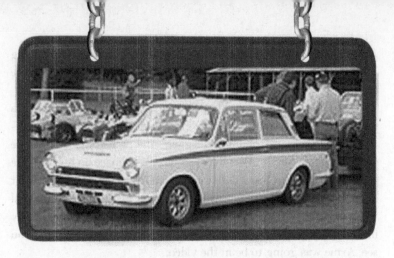

Lotus Cortina Mk1

HOW TO CRASH YOUR FIRST RACE CAR

"Taxi!" shouted the cheeky idiot parked next to me on the starting line. He was in a stunningly prepared Porsche 356.

I shouted back, "I'll fuckin' taxi you, ya cheeky twat." That got me my first warning from the marshal, that bad language was not part of racing. "Oh bollocks," I said. Then he warned me again. But I went out anyway, looking for Mr. Porsche. Found him, scared him, and myself. And I found out the Cortina is a brick with wheels. How did racing legends like Jim Clark and the others do it in the sixties? I'd bought a video and watched them. It was easy: to go fast 'round a corner, all you have to do is turn in under-braking. This will get the car on two wheels. Slide the tail out while you have the opposite lock on, then as soon as the windscreen's in line with the rest of the road, you straighten her up and off you go, having kept your foot on the throttle all the way through. Scary, but loads of fun.

Anyway, my first race was a one-hour enduro at Road Atlanta in 1998, and off I go. The blue sky turns black. I've heard about Georgia downpours, but never seen one. It starts to rain. I mean, it's pissing down. I have dry tires on. I call Thomas Rantzow, my crew chief. "Mate, I can't see because we have no wipers, and I'm sliding off the road."

Thomas has a wonderful smile, but hardly uses it, in case somebody thinks he's nice.

Thomas to Brian: "You've only got one lap to go and you're first in class and fifth overall. Just take it easy."

Brian to Thomas: "I am taking it easy, because I can't see."

Thomas to Brian: "Well, you should know your way around by now."

It was at that moment that I hit the bridge at about 90 mph. Rolled over and over and landed on my side. First race—first crash. The flag marshal pulled me out and I lay on the side of the track, thinking, "Helicopter ride!" When the medic came, he told me not to move.

I looked at him and said, "You're gay."

He said, "I know, silly. Just relax."

Turned out I was fine. Thomas was a little upset, because he'd just built the car, and it was well bashed, but we could rebuild. Then out of the gloom came this huge Dually pickup truck. It was my buddy Jesse James Dupree, the singer with the band Jackyl, who lived nearby and had prepared lunch. I kid you not, in the back of the truck was a whole barbecued pig and all the trimmings. He and I and the whole team sat, drank beer, and ate pig around the Cortina. You can't make shit like this up. After that day, I am hooked forever.

From Bedfords to Bedknobs

BUILDING A CAR WITH A HEADBOARD

One of the ways we had fun in the fifties was filling in *I-Spy* books, which were spotters' guides for kids. Each book covered a different subject, things like cars. Whenever you saw a car (or a tree, or a plane), you ticked it off, then you sent in the book and got a certificate.

Being a car nut, I wanted to "spy" Daimler Conquests, Mercedes, and Admirals. Where were they? Perhaps in the posh areas; like the streets of Newcastle were full of them, because Dunston's sure weren't.

It was around this time that people started buying TVs. The job of digging up the streets and installing the cables for the TVs was given to a contractor called Rediffusion. Fleets of red Bedfords drove up and down Britain. As soon as we clapped eyes on these vans, we were determined to get in one. They were so new and fabulous to us.

I'll never forget it.

My first smell of gasoline was the smell of freedom. When I told Pops about the vans, he knew the only way he was going to have some peace was if he got me driving. He wasn't a sergeant major for nothing. So off he went to the local garage and asked them if they had an old steering wheel. It could come from any car as long as it wasn't German. He got one for sixpence (I didn't get any pocket money that week). He got a large stick, pushed it through our headboard, and piled all the pillows up, like a driving seat.

"Son, there's your first car," he said. Four legs, iron castors, no brakes, no gas tank, no tax, no insurance. "Thanks, Pops." I jumped in and drove forever. It was everything I'd ever wanted. As Pops left the room, I heard him mutter, "Thank Christ for that . . ."

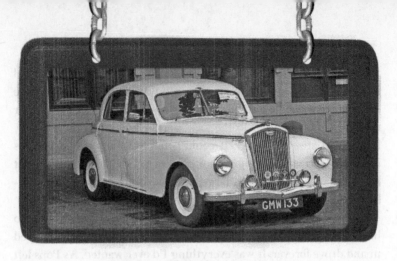

The Wolseley

MY FIRST LOVE

I'll never forget the day my dad said, "C'mon, youse two," to me and my brother, Maurice. It was summer 1959, a beautiful Saturday morning. "We're going to Byker," he said. That was on the other side of Newcastle. We didn't know why we were going, but it was unusual.

Off we went on the number 66 bus—the Dunston circular, it was called. Then to Marlborough Crescent bus station, and then Newcastle City Transport to Byker. At the top of Byker Road, there was a used-car garage called Northern Motors, and we were heading straight for it.

Now, it couldn't be he was going to buy a car, not my dad. Maybe he was just gonna buy me another steering wheel. His face was set like stone. My heart was beating fast. Look at these cars all around me! Oh my God, a Nash Metropolitan, yellow-and-white. Dad went straight to a dark green Wolseley 6/90, long hood, six cylinders, beautiful. I couldn't breathe.

"Can I have a test drive?" he asked the salesman.

"No," the man replied, "but I'll turn it over for you." The engine started on the button. My old man said, "I'll take it." We were gonna have a car. Well, I was. You see, in my head, it was mine, all mine. I, little Brian Johnson, was going to be a nonpedestrian, a motorist. I could learn how to work all the buttons and sticklike things and find out what they do, and then I could go to technical college and sit my exams to become a taxi driver. It was written in the stars. Walt Disney was right: "When you wish upon a star, you will get your motorcarrr!"

"Is there something wrong with your lad?" I heard the salesman say.

My father said, "He's bloody car-daft. C'mon, youse two." Then, to me, "Not there, in the back. I've gotta drive." The thing was, my dad's driving license was an army one, and he hadn't driven anything since the Second World War—and that was a three-ton truck. This car had column-shift gears and an ignition key; the wind-down windows were something of a novelty, too. Every time we tried to talk or ask a question, he would say, "Shurrup! I'm trying to drive." That didn't instill much confidence. After about thirty minutes, he had gone mad. He started singing, "I'm lost, I'm lost. I don't know where I am," at the top of his voice, just like a demented black-and-white minstrel. It took us one and a half hours to do a half-hour journey. By the time we got home, he was sweating and exhausted and walked one and a half miles to the social club for a beer. The car was parked outside our house, 1 Beech Drive. It was ours! Not the doctor's, not the banker's or the landlord's. Mine!

Dad had left the door open. I climbed in and got behind the wheel. It was twelve forty-five in the afternoon; at six thirty in the evening, they were still trying to pry my fingers from the steering wheel, my eyes glazed wide-open. You see, I was still on the road, somewhere in my imagination. They finally got me in the house, but I just sat on the windowsill looking at the car. As you can see in the photograph, I was in love for the first time in my life. Twelve years old and already spoken for.

Dad took us for drives in the country, and we just loved it—not the countryside, the drives. He'd take us to a beautiful place called "the Meeting of the Waters," where the North Tyne and South Tyne meet. Once we got there, Mam would put out a blanket and set out a picnic, but I would be behind the wheel, going somewhere else, where there was no school, no foul weather, where the air smelled of leather, gasoline, and wood, and where time was not a thief.

P.S.: The car lived with us for about two years, until my father couldn't really afford the repairs and the gas. Then, one day, it was gone, just like that. My father never bought another car for the rest of his life, nor did he ever drive one again. If that Wolseley still exists, I'll buy it. Name your price.

Grand National

THE RACE THAT STOPPED A COUNTRY

One of my great memories as a kid is of the Grand National. Everything in Great Britain stopped to watch this race. I put my very first bet on, a whole week's pocket and milk-round money, about three shillings, and, to this day, I don't know why I did. I bet on a gray horse called Merryman II. It won. I screamed, shouted, "Hallowed be thy mane!" I had money. About two pounds. Boy, it was a lot then! I went straight to the toy shop and bought an Aston Martin AC3 race car, all green and English, and a green double-decker bus I'd had my eye on. And last but not least, a Mosquito fighter plastic model airplane kit. I was keen on the smell of the glue (er, just kidding . . .).

Childhood memories are great. You just remember them as you get older. And you're ashamed you ever lost them.

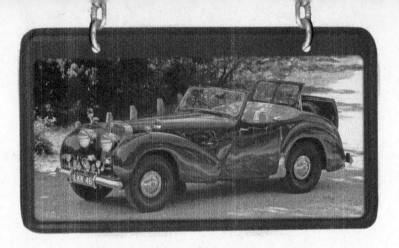

The Bulldog and the Chick

WHEN AN OLD BRIT SHAGS A BEAUTIFUL ITALIAN

Four years after getting the AC/DC gig, I bought my first Triumph Roadster. It was metallic green, with those beautiful rumble seats and a second windshield for the passengers. It wasn't the fastest car on the planet, but it looked mighty cool with those huge chrome headlights. I loved it so much that I shipped it to America.

My fondest memory is of Cliff Williams coming to see me in his new Ferrari Mondial. Oh, he was a proud man, standing there with his scarlet prancing horse. But when it came to starting it, his horse wouldn't dance. It was stone fucking dead.

I got some jump cables and stuck them up its arse. The joy of connecting a 1948 Triumph to a brand-new Ferrari and watching it come to life was unforgettable. Cliff was a little embarrassed, but you should have seen the smile on the Triumph's face. The old British bulldog had just shagged a beautiful Italian chick.

Cliff never had much luck with Ferraris. A couple years later, he picked one up brand-new from Fort Lauderdale, and was driving it back to Fort Myers, when he smelled something funny. He stopped and called the dealership, they said it was the newness of the engine, so off he went again. About five miles down the road, he didn't smell anything, but he did see flames in his rearview mirror. He stopped, jumped out, sat down, lit a fag, and watched his lovely new Ferrari burn into a red mud. He never bought another one.

I sold my Triumph to William Kelly (or Billy, as everyone knows him), the famous painter who is Sister Wendy's favorite artist. Why I sold it is quite sad. When Billy's mother was in Sarasota, on her last visit before she died, she loved the car so much she asked me to take her for a drive, which I did, the whole length of Siesta Key, with the top down, the beautiful sunshine, the Gulf of Mexico and white sand. She sat by me with a smile on her face, saying nothing. Her eyes spoke volumes—her youth, her first love, whatever—it was just a beautiful moment in a beautiful car with a beautiful lady. It was the last time I saw her.

Six months later, Billy asked me if I would part with the car, because, he said, it was all his mother had talked about after the ride, and it would always remind him of her. I did just that, and he drives it now with his big old straw hat—you can't miss him on Siesta Key. And who's that sitting beside him? Naaah, it couldn't be.

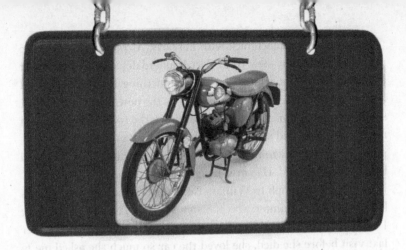

The BSA Bantam

THE OPPOSITE OF A CHICK MAGNET

My very first means of motorized transport was an ex-army, khaki-colored BSA 125-cc Bantam. My father had bought it off a friend at work. It was almost brand-new. This friend had bought an ex-army Bedford three-ton truck at an auction. It had a canvas cover on the back. He took it home, and under the canvas were ten motorcycles, part of a job lot. So he sold them to workmates and it paid for the truck and then some.

Once again, my dad was thinking of me, not himself. The bike was a typical piece of British "why we nearly lost the war" lump of shite. I mean, what would you rather go to war in? A BMW or an Austin? A Mercedes or a Morris? Everything on this bike smacked of the First World War. The accelerator cable snapped at least once a week. The headlight bulbs popped at any speed over 35 mph. This was the mechanical equivalent of rubbing one out while wearing a boxing glove.

It had a single-seat spring-loaded saddle, which looked like it had been on a horse in a western at one time. There was no battery—

everything worked off the (very dodgy) dynamo. Oh yeah, and it had a kick start that didn't kick. When, and if, it started, it sounded like a squadron of bees flying low. With popping noises that sounded like ack-ack guns firing at them. It had three gears and a potluck gearbox. This was about as basic as it got. Riding to work was an adventure, especially on freezing-cold mornings. I had to go down a cobbled street called Forth Banks, which led to the Quayside. There was a sharp left-hander at the bottom. Icy cobbles and skinny tires are not good together, and every other morning I'd slide and end up under the bike. But I wasn't the only one. There were lots of other blokes under their bikes, too. I made a lot of friends lying on the road under my BSA bike.

"Hey, mate, you all right?"

"Oh aye, lad. I think it's my knee today. I did my ankle and me flask of tea yesterday." We'd help each other up and continue on our way. I tried to tart my bike up by painting it black and silver, only to find that enamel paint reacts pretty badly with army khaki—it bubbled up so that the bike looked like a loofah with wheels on. This bike was not a chick magnet. Even old crones would titter as I pootled past.

The final straw was when I went for a ride one Sunday to Rowlands Gill. I was about three miles past Swalwell when the chain came off. After an hour of fiddling, I got it back on. Then the accelerator cable snapped again. I pushed the bastard seven miles home—mainly uphill with the odd down.

BSA stands for Birmingham Small Arms. I wish they had stuck to doing that. I can't grumble too much, though. It did get me from A to B. From the pedestrian-slicing front license plate to the rear light, which came on when it felt like it, and the oil dripping from the engine casing, it was kinda cute in a "we'll fight them on the beaches" sorta way.

Now, the Mods were coming to power, and scooters were the thing. Lambrettas and Vespas with loads of mirrors; parka coats with fur edging on the hood; and The Who. I was being left behind by "my generation." I had to move quickly. I gave the bike away to a friend—who never spoke to me again.

A Lovely Story

HOW NOT TO ORDER ROOM SERVICE

Sit, my fellow car nuts, whilst I tell a story about a good friend. Is he a race driver? Is he a musician? I cannot tell, for he is a married man still, "still" being the operative word. My friend found himself in Singapore, and he treated himself to a night in the Peninsula Hotel, a very beautiful place. He went to his room. "Ah, what a view!" he thought.

It was about seven thirty in the evening when he started getting a little edgy in the penis and wanting-a-shag department. He picked up the phone book and did the natural thing: he looked under "escorts." He phoned the number, and a sexy lady's voice said, "Can I help you, sir?"

He said, "Yes, I want two gorgeous girls who are into each other and want to do me, too. I don't mind a little kinky stuff, either, a few whips and handcuffs. And I do expect them to shag each other."

The lady on the phone said softly, "Sir, you have to dial 9 for an outside line."

He did not sleep well that night.

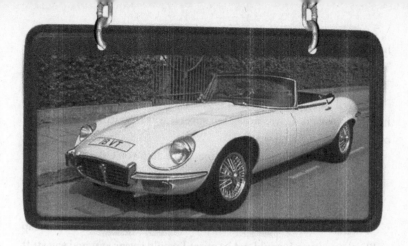

The E-Type Penis Extension

TOO HOT TO RUN

I first met Thomas Rantzow in Sarasota, Florida, in 1988. I was buying a 1973 Jaguar V12 E-Type. It was automatic; in fact, that's all they sold in the U.S. Anyway, Thomas had built this one up himself. It was silver with cherry-red upholstery, with stunningly lowered suspension and huge fat tires. It was also an accident waiting to happen. E-Types didn't like it much when you turned on your headlights, air con, windscreen wipers, and radio at the same time, and would basically call it quits. Why? Lucas electrics, England's finest. In America, Lucas was called the "Prince of Darkness." It was the auto union of electrics.

But that was by the by. The XKE, as Americans call them, was gorgeous, and I was driving this beautiful penis extension down to Fort Myers, where I lived at the time. I didn't even make it to the interstate before some strange, banging noises came from under the hood. I phoned the garage and they sent out Thomas. They sent Thomas out so many times after that that we became friends, and Thomas, as you know, became our race-team chief.

I loved to drive that E-Type, when it wasn't broken, or pretending to be broken. It was alive, I'm sure. It was a pouting, spoiled brat of a car.

Phone call to Thomas: "Hey, mate, the Jag won't start."

Thomas: "Are you sure? Don't give it too much gas."

Brian: "Thomas, I just turned the friggin' key, and it wouldn't start."

Thomas: "Okay, I'll be right over."

Thomas would come, sit in it, turn the key once, and it would leap to life. Sometimes I would get so upset I would swear at it and say stuff like "Lada," "Polski Fiat," "Yugo," just to piss it off. The pick of the litter in E-Types was certainly the straight 6, early sixties model. What a shape! And who can forget three of them getting chucked over a cliff in *The Italian Job*? That brought a tear to a generation's eyes. If you owned an E-Type, you couldn't really say to someone, "I'll be there at seven," because you'd never make it. The trouble with E-Types was they just couldn't be bothered to putz around city streets, it made them overheat something terrible. Believe me, I went through three radiators.

My brother-in-law, Dr. Arild Jacobson, loved the E-Type, and visits us every year from Norway. He'd asked me for years about buying it. I finally relented in 2005. He shipped it to Norway, where, he says, it runs like a dream, because "it's cold there." So that was the problem! It was too hot where I lived in Florida. Simple, eh?

The next time we visited Arild and family was summer 2006, up in their mountain home in Beitostølen, and I had missed the Jag more than I cared to admit. Arild asked me if I would like to drive it down to the town. I said yes please, and as I drove down those beautiful mountain roads, I suddenly got it. The orgasmic exhaust noise, the long, sexy hood (penis extension), the not-very-good brakes (penis retraction and "pucker factor" on mountain roads). It seemed to be saying to me, "I told you, dickhead, it was too bloody hot." Then, when we arrived at the town center, I parked, and the radiator hissed, farted slightly, and took a huge dump, gallons of water pouring from out of the thing.

Arild smiled and said, "I think it's too hot today!"

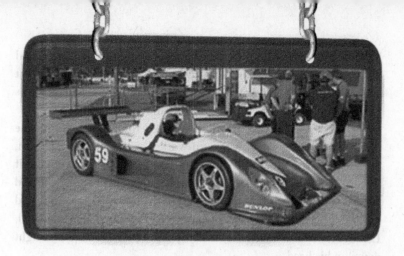

The Pilbeam

A LOT MORE TIT FOR YOUR BANG

In February 2008, I drove my first race in the Pilbeam MP84. My wife, Brenda, had bought it for my fifty-ninth birthday, God love her. I had to wait a year to race it, because it was a giant leap from the Royale RP4. I went to test it and practice with it with Sasco Sports, who look after it at the stunning Virginia raceway. I must admit, the buttons and computer thingies everywhere were daunting, but I had to prove I could drive it so's I could get my Super License from Historic Sports-car Racing and go from group three to group six, where there's a big leap in driver performance. Maybe it was asking too much of myself—it was like going from Twiggy to Pamela Anderson, a lot more tit for your bang.

It was the 4 Hours of Sebring again. Dave Handy, the Sasco boss, would do the first forty-six minutes, I would drive the next fifty minutes, Pete Argetsinger would do thirty-five minutes in the middle, and I'd do the last session. That was the plan, anyway. Another gorgeous day. Twelve noon start. I'm looking forward to this, but I see the other cars practicing. Oh my God, "Spices," Lola, Judd

V10s—this wasn't vintage anymore, this was the real deal with real pro drivers. I was in for an almighty ass-kicking, but ya gotta start somewhere. Why couldn't it be a nice, smooth track like Watkins Glen, Road Atlanta, Road America, or Lime Rock?

By the second day of practice, I started to fall in love with the car. It was quicker than a shipyard worker at the four o'clock siren, quicker than shit off a shiny shovel. Wow, this thing could go! But it was the stopping that really got your attention. Every time you had to pick your eyeballs off your chest. The G-force was something I'd never experienced before. The team were great boys, Virginians all; Les wore a walrus mustache, red suspenders, and a hat pulled tight down on his head.

It was race day. At eight thirty in the morning, I went to our paddock, and there was my gearbox in pieces. What the hell! "Les!" "Les! Les!" He was drinking coffee and reading the paper. "Les, there's only three and a half hours to go, mate." He looked up and said, "Morning y'all, Mr. Brian. Sit down, I got some fresh cornbread. I gotta get the dog rings on the shaft a while and put this puppy back together in about one hour tops, okay?" and started reading his paper again. Of course, he was right. Just like the "predator" team, these guys were pros and I was a nervous girl. The car looked just magnificent.

I was in group three of group six. Groups one and two were V10s and V12s, fast, vicious buggers driven by fast, vicious buggers. These guys didn't take prisoners and they didn't care that it was my first race with the car. At the drivers' meeting, Ken Fengler, chief dude at HSR, introduced me: "Gentlemen, you have fresh meat today . . . Oh, I'm sorry . . . You have a first-time Super License–holder today. Try and keep an eye on him!" Well, that made me feel just like a live rabbit at a greyhound track. And I was English—even better! The German guys didn't care where I was from; they were after ze whole vorld anyway.

The race was getting nearer and I was getting nervouser. The flag dropped, the bullshit stopped, and Dave Handy was away in a field of forty-five cars. We'd qualified seventh, which was brilliant: against these cars, our engine was a Nissan V6, the smallest. I was sitting waiting my turn. It was hot in my suit, and the cars were going by so fast. I thought, "Jeez, I'm going out into that!" This was a different world. "Okay, you're in!"

In comes Dave and the car goes up on hydraulic jacks. I pop in. Shit, it's a spaceship! I've forgotten everything I've learned. The new tires are going on, we're refueling— Oooh this is Formula 1 shit. The car goes down and I'm off. Don't stall, don't stall. I don't. Yeah! Yeehaw! Hubble-bubblaflubbla-flibble-wibbly, I forgot to put my visor down. I just got out, and the flag marshal was waving blue at me; that means someone's going to pass you. I was blue-flagged all the way 'round and I never saw the guy behind me. I came back 'round to the first flag, still waving, and I shouted, "Go flag yourself!" I never did see what they saw, because nothing passed me until the big boys came 'round.

Then it happened. The car in front that I was trying to take dropped something—a bolt?—straight into my rear tire. It blew the thing up at about 145 mph. The car wallowed sideways, the wall was coming nearer, and I had a bowel movement or two. I saw Heaven, and it looked dull. I was back again—I'd controlled the car! All that was left was the outer rim of the tire, which was going in and out from the bodywork like a licorice allsort having a shag. "Oh bollocks, I gotta make it back to the pit!" Thankfully, it held; crew waiting, new tire. Go, go, go!

Off again, everything running good. I check my computer readouts. It's tough at the start, but then you get used to it, like getting used to women who stop giving blow jobs the instant they're married. I see my suspension cantilever didendum slatulisor is going well, and my rear-brake induction certainty levels are right up there. Then Wally Dallenbach goes by. The noise of my engine and his together causes this strange sensation in my head. It's not Cilla again; it feels like someone's frozen a footlong corn on the cob and pushed it in one ear and pulled it out the other, a scraping-of-nails-on-the-blackboard thing. Shit! There was fluid on my visor—where the hell was that coming from? I was out of tear-offs, so I wiped it off with the back of my glove. I looked down and saw my suit was covered with a thin layer of foam all the way up from my legs. "What the fuck?" I panicked a little. Was this some acid eating away at my suit?

It is my last lap before Pete takes it. I do a really quick lap and I'm in the pits. I jump out; people are pointing at me, my crew's hosing me down, the cockpit's full of foam. Dave comes running back. "It's okay. The fire extinguisher went off." Pete gets in the car and he's off. "Go on, Pete, my son, we haven't lost any time." What had happened was the two engine noises were powerful enough to vibrate the onboard fire bottle to "on." See, I told you it was a friggin' strange noise! Pete does some great driving and we're lying about fifth. Wow! Top ten, not bad, not bad at all.

When I'm back in, he tells me, "Brian, it's getting like glass out there. Take it easy, don't snap the gas. Easy, smooth, okay?" "Okay," I say. This is what all the hard work's been for, this fifty minutes or so. I'm starting to feel my neck and arm muscles; my, that G-force is a little bastard. "Don't do anything wrong, son," I tell myself. One of the strange things about racing on a track like Sebring is it's 3.7 miles long, and for the first twenty minutes I never saw another car. "Where the hell is everybody?" It gave me a chance, on my own, with nothing to hold me up.

Then, all of a sudden, just like a jam on the M6 road, the whole friggin' world's there. "Now, be careful, kidda. Take your time." After many mini-adventures, the checkered flag dropped. This time, I knew the boy done good; the whole team was up on the wall, the marshals cheering. Straight into the winners' circle. Third overall, first in class, first index of performance, three cups, and three visits to the podium. I gave the crew the first-in-class cup for the factory. God, I smiled a lot. I'd done it in my first race! I was pumped, happier than a dog with two cocks. And I never said "fuck" once in the interview.

On the podium, this very young professional German driver who'd won the race overall looked at me. "You are Brine Chunsen! Zis iss not pazzibol. You are ze zinker wis ze AC unt zu DC. How iss it pazzibol zat yu are up mein schvartzepoofen fur der whole raze? You are tu ault for zis."

"Watch it, bonny lad!" I said. "That was me first race. You'll be lookin' up my poopenchuten when I get the hang of this car."

"No, vait! You must giff me an outogram. This was a bit more like it." He paused. "For my muzzer. Ha, ha, ha!"

Cheeky twat! He was actually trying to be friendly; it's just that German humor's not humorous to anyone but Germans.

A German friend of mine, Ralph Kellener, is a great professional driver: Le Mans twenty-four-hour, Daytona, etc., etc. Gunther the Demon Driver told me a joke once: "Brine, vy do chermen men like new carss?" "I don't know, Gunther. Why?" He was laughing so hard whilst trying to deliver the punch line: "Because zey luf virchins unt ze smell of lezzer." Bemused, I pulled out my Luger and shot him in the German funny bone—that's the bit between the eyes. He said it smarted a bit, but you can't keep an old German driver down. Do you know they don't have a word for nipples in Germany?

They're called chest warts. *"Gervospriktechknicker."*

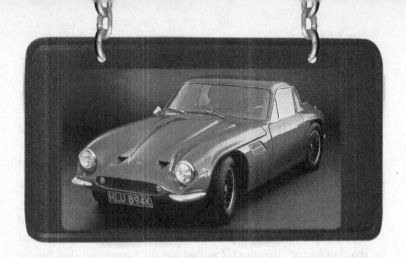

TVR

TWO SEATS AND A SHELF

Every band had one, and Tom Hill was Geordie's. Tom Hill was our bass player and, like everyone, he had a hobby. His was money, so parting with it meant a lot to him. One day, in London, he saw an ad for a TVR Griffith, and he went to see it, and me and the drummer Brian Gibson tagged along. I can't remember the engine size, but I'm sure it was a Ford 1.6-liter engine. Built in Wales, it was a snazzy-looking fiberglass sports car, two seats and a shelf. Tom Hill bought the car, I sat on the shelf, and Brian Gibson in the passenger seat, and we drove back to our glamorous council flat, you'd call them projects, in Hackney (not a place to be in 1973).

As we were driving back, the most incredible thing happened. The horn button sprang like a snake on speed straight into Tom's face, and it sounded like it hurt. Did the car know something? I've had a soft spot for TVRs ever since.

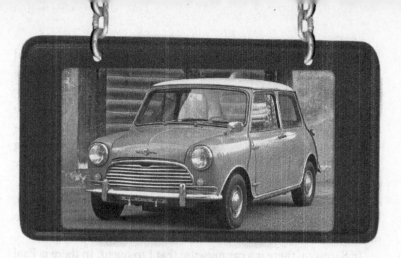

The Mini

THE BEATLES OF CARS

I suppose the coolest car I had when I was young was my Mini. It was white with a black roof. It was an Austin, thirdhand, with sliding windows and a floor start (but it actually started, unlike the Ford Popular I was used to). I loved that car. It was the sixties, and I was in the Beatles of motorcars. I could go to parties and not have to hide my old "Pop" 'round the back of the house. I could say "fab" and mean it. It would always get me to work on time. It had a heater that heated, wipers that wiped, and a built-in smileometer. I had GT go-faster stripes on the bottom of the doors and a pretend Cooper S exhaust, which made it sound fast even though it was under 1000 cc. So, basically, it was like trying to polish a turd, but I didn't give a flying fart—it looked the part.

Sexual adventures in the backseat took on an acrobatic quality. After about two months, I could have joined the Royal Ballet, although I did lock a testicle once. As I've mentioned, the sliding front windows were designed for shagging only (it's where the ankles exited)—because they weren't much good for anything else.

A lot of girls affected the Dusty Springfield hairstyle then, and the hairspray they used came straight from the chemical-warfare lab. So if you didn't want to lose an eye, motorcycle goggles were always a good option. The hairspray fumes made it very unsafe to fart within three feet of the said hair, so a small fire blanket was always handy, too. But the worst thing was that guys were splashing themselves with Brut and Old Spice aftershave. Which contained the other ingredients the hairspray needed to form napalm.

The Mini changed a whole generation. That's some statement, but it's true. It won rallies, especially the Monte Carlo. It was a joy to drive—and the memories keep coming back.

In Sarasota, there is a car museum that I frequent. In there is Paul McCartney's Mini and the Beatles' first Bentley. I often have a sit in the Mini when no one's about and start singing, "There are places I remember . . ."

The new Mini is a wonderful car—the Germans got it just right. But for me, when it's standing next to the original, it's the sixties one I want to drive. It's got that "we've got the best bands in the world, Union Jack, buy British, see you in the King's Road, 'Jumpin' Jack Flash,' 'My Generation,' Ban the Bomb, England 4–Germany 2" feel about it. Paddy Hopkirk was a national treasure, and he starred with his rally-winning Mini on *Sunday Night at the London Palladium*—the only car to ever headline a TV variety show. Geddin' there!

Phil Rudd

OCCUPATION: WORLD'S BEST DRUMMER

You'll usually see Phil driving alone, the reason being everyone is too scared to get in the car with him. You see, Phil thinks all the other cars on the road are there for his entertainment. The rest of the lads would make all kinds of excuses; mine was, "Sorry, mate, I've got to stay home and rearrange my fridge magnets." Undeterred, he would venture out looking for other band members. Angus's excuse was that he'd forgotten the riff to "Highway to Hell" and had to practice it again. Cliff feigned endless nausea attacks, and Mal just said, "You're fucking joking."

Phil loves racing, though, and has a saloon race car in New Zealand, one of the big V8 jobs, but we'll get to that later. Phil's first exotic was a Ferrari 308 GTB—red, of course. I was riding with him (he'd used ether to get me in) and we were ripping up the A1. It was a chain drive, and something was wrong with it; it sounded like Big Ben on acid, steroids, and a large dollop of cocaine—until it broke. He sold it broken, and bought a series of exotics that were legend then. But Phil being Phil, he wanted them now.

One night in 1983, we were going to do a big show at the Birmingham NEC, a huge monstrosity of English design. It looked a bit like a Second World War airfield, with no bombers and no war, and as charming as Idi Amin. One hour to showtime. "Where's Phil?" someone asked.

"He's driving up from London in his new car," said Jones the Drum, Phil's drum tech. (He was Welsh. Still is, actually.)

I said, "What kind of car is it?"

"He never told me," said Jones the Drum.

"Holy crap! Thirty minutes to showtime—where the hell is he?" The crowd was getting revved up; it was a sellout gig. What worried us was the weather. There was the mother of all rainstorms out there, and the M6 is notorious for its switchbacks.

Then, suddenly, the back doors opened and in roared Phil, in a genuine red Ford GT40, tires completely shot and him soaked to the skin. The tires were shot because he'd been low-level flying at about 140 mph all the way. He was soaked because the doors on the beast retract into the roof so you can get in and they don't have adequate rubber seals to keep water out. Boy, can that guy make an entrance!

The car just glistened backstage, as did Phil. No one really cared that we only had fifteen minutes to go; we just ogled, leered, cheered, sniffed tires and brakes—all cooking nicely. There was a heat haze coming from the engine. Then the huge AC/DC bell descended from the rafters. "DONG!" it went. "Shit, we're on!"

Then there was the BMW M1. What a beautiful car! Phil bought one and immediately found its flaws: yeah, yeah, the driver got pretty much cooked. You received an engine enema while driving. But Phil didn't care. We were recording in Paris—"I'm going to drive the M1 there," he said. "I'll be there by teatime."

Once again, he was late, and we were getting worried. He got there about nine P.M. "Bollocks! Shit! Fuck! Piss!"

"Trouble?" I inquired.

"I was on the *périphérique* and stopped to get gas. I looked at the pumps: *benzole* or *benzine,* and I fill it up with *benzole.* It's fucking diesel. FUCKING DIESEL!"

That one took a couple of weeks to fix. Phil went on to own a Ferrari Daytona 365 GTB, 512 BB; he's raced Fiestas 'round Europe and now races in New Zealand in a V8 Commodore. Oh yeah, and he's the best rock 'n' roll drummer in the world.

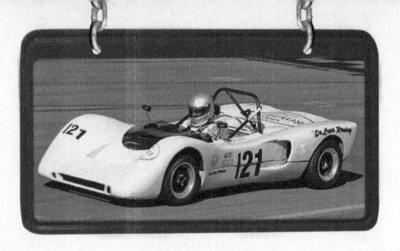

Sebring

"DOES ROSE KENNEDY HAVE A BLACK DRESS?"

Sebring. One of the legendary tracks in the world, hard on the car, brutal on the driver, and a crippler on the wallet. It is without doubt the bumpiest, nastiest, and most fabulous race track in the world. The town of Sebring is, well, not anything at all really. I mean, when a Chili's wins "Best Place to Eat" five years in a row, you know you are pretty much fucked.

But I just love the place. It was, and still is, an airfield. It was used in the Second World War to train RAF pilots and is used now to train wannabe race-car drivers during the week.

I was here to drive in the three-hour enduro, for 2.5 liters and under. My ride was a Royale RP4 built in England a long time ago, but fear not, I did do my best for queen and country. I had modified this beautiful little car myself. Thomas, my trusty Swede, was at my side the night before practice. He was by my side because, if I had moved, he would have fallen down. He was very drunk, in preparation for a long weekend.

As dawn broke over Sebring, the mist cleared to reveal the most beautiful sight to these eyes—racing cars everywhere. Gorgeous, exotic, and all fucking German, except mine and a couple of Japanese jobs. There was the sound of groans from the pit crews who'd nudged the turps slightly the night before, and then my personal favorite: the toilets. The groans and farting from the cubicles, watching the toes of sneakers curling up, wait for it, the log hitting the water—splash—then "ahhhh." And the sneakers coming out under the door. There won't be any arse-wiping for a while, well, not until they're rested. Remember, this is not Formula 1! Moving on . . .

I get suited and booted for the eight thirty practice session, and find out I must have a codriver for the race. It's in the rules. Bugger, now I *am* in trouble. "Thomas, mate," I announce, "we need another driver or we are screwed."

Thomas was under the car, and all I could see were his feet. I figured he was busy, so off I went in search of a codriver, with as much chance of a Sunday dinner in Ethiopia. But there, walking up the pit lane, was Pete Argetsinger.

No, I didn't make it up, that's his name. And a bloody good driver he is, too.

Me: "Pete, me old tart, me old pal, how's it hanging?"

Him: "Who are you?"

Me: "It's me, Brian. Brian Johnson. Oh, you know."

Him: "Nope."

Then he winked and gave me one of those punches in the arm which make you want to deck the bugger.

Me: "You wanna codrive with me, mate?"

Then he said these immortal words: "Does Rose Kennedy have a black dress?"

And he was on board. I rushed back to tell Thomas. "Thomas, mate, listen, good news . . ." Hold on, he's still under the car. Not trouble, I hope . . . I looked under. The guy was fast asleep. That's where he'd crawled the night before and he'd never moved.

Okay, Johnson, me boy, I said to myself, you've got the smallest engine in the race, 1300 cc, and you've got one of the oldest cars in the race, you don't have any rain tires because Thomas doesn't think it's gonna rain, and this is your very first three hours in this car. You don't know if the engine will hold for three hours and, to top it all, you are pretty much an old fart yourself. And last but not least, a Geordie has never won here. Right, well, I'm quite optimistic! Thomas, out from underneath the Royale, cracks a smile. I know he knows something I don't.

We do quite well in practice—Pete says the car's driving well but, like me, he knows we have a battle on our hands. Porsches, 2 and 2.5 liters, very fast and in very capable hands. So we decide to just enjoy the race and see how far our little English car can take us.

Race day. It's a nine A.M. till noon race (the big boys race the afternoon three-hour). Pete Argetsinger says to me, "I'll take it out first session, try to get a comfortable position and bed the car in."

"Hmm!" I think. What if it doesn't last that long? I won't even get a drive. But I bow to his judgment.

Green flag: They're off. We had qualified twelfth on the grid out of forty cars—not bad for a littl'un. The hour seemed to drag by, then Thomas shouted, "Helmet on, he's coming in."

This is it! Don't get nervous, me son. Stay focused. Oh Christ, I've just noticed my underpants have crawled up my arse again. Too late. I've got $50 Calvin Kleins on and $35 are stuck up my chimney. (Why am I telling you this? I'm writing out loud again, must stop that.) In Pete roars, jumps out, refuel, quick, quick, in you get, seat adjustment, don't forget the bottom belt that goes up your crotch. (The one that makes your balls go bang.)

Okay, I'm in. Gloves on, visor down, switch on, ignition, fire it up, waved away. Go! Go! Go! And I'm off! Sebring turn one is a nasty fast corner that goes from four lanes down to two. Oh yeah, and it's a blind one! I gradually come up to speed, and it turns out to be one of those days when everything is right—drivers call it "being in the zone." I was one with the car, nothing passed me, and I kept passing cars. Back markers? I didn't know. In enduros, it's notoriously difficult to tell who's winning. I just kept driving. I come in for fuel. Thomas just looks grim. I think he thinks the car isn't going to last, or maybe he's just enjoying himself. Honestly, you never knew.

Out again, the corners come and go. The cars keep coming and I keep overtaking. The heels of my race boots stick to the floor with the rubber coming from the cars in front. So I basically heel-and-toe my way 'round (that's driver talk for being a smart-arse).

Checkered flag, go past the pits. Thomas and Pete are standing on the pit wall, Pete clapping, Thomas smiling! Sweden must have put their first man on the moon or dropped to second in the suicide league tables. I drive back to our paddock. Take off my helmet, nobody there. Then I hear on the Tannoy, "Will Brian Johnson please come to the winners' circle?"

Shit! I had to start the car again. Trouble was, I didn't know how to get there. Finally, with much frantic waving and flapping of arms, the marshals got me there. Everybody was clapping and smiling. Did I get a podium? Must've done. I jumped out the car.

"First overall."

"No, that's not right."

"Yup, you are, mate," said Pete, which was nice of him, seeing as how he drove with me.

We climbed the podium. I was elated, as you can tell in the photograph. The first Geordie boy to win at Sebring. I'll check just in case. Anyway, the first Geordie boy with Italian blood in him to win the three-hour.

I was interviewed live on the radio and racetrack Tannoy after the presentation and the shaking of the champagne bottle. I was later told I said "fuck" eleven times. That's fuckin' awful.

My Dad and Mam

TRYING TO REPAY A DEBT

I guess I took for granted my father's sense of my love of anything motorized. He seemed to know that I was destined for something other than working down a mine, but he was a tough, hard man and couldn't show his affection in any way, shape, or form. No hugs, no smiles, no contact. Just: "Here, I got you this"—a 1959 Ford Popular "sit up and beg" for £50, which was a lot of money to him. The car was nothing to most men. To me, it was my freedom. To him, it was all he had and it was all his love. I wish he was alive to see me race. To see me win.

I'll never win like he did, and he never won a thing but me.

I tried to repay them for the rest of my life. I did the rock-star thing and bought them a house, but not the big one I wanted to buy. They wanted to pick their own. Their address is still in my phone book: "Mam and Dad, 82 Mountside Gdns, Dunston. Tel.: 91-4606137." That was the place they loved. It looked over the Tyne and Newcastle. It's where the "well-off" lived, they said. They were happy there, and so was I when I visited them. When you looked out of the window, you looked down on a house—No. 1 Oak Avenue— right into the window where I was born on October 5, 1947. No! They couldn't have? But it's true. My mam, Esther Maria Octavia De Luca, and my dad, Alan Johnson, bought a house overlooking the bedroom I was born in. With parents like that, you've got it made.

Mam was soft with us, everything Dad wasn't. She spoiled us with nothing but love, because she didn't have anything else. She had come from a wealthy family in Frascati, Rome, to a council house with a view of Scotswood Road. She'd make extra money making wedding dresses; she was a brilliant dressmaker. We kids went to sleep to the sound of her sewing machine, pedal variety. I don't have words for this lady. And lady is what she was. She died of an aneurysm in 1998 and didn't know who we were. I was sick of crying when she died.

And I'm one of what's left of them. And every corner of every racetrack I drive is named after them—in my head, anyway. *Gotta stop now.*

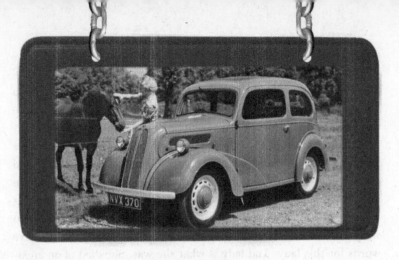

Popular

KING OF THE ROAD

The 1959 Ford Popular left a little to be desired. It had a three-speed gearbox with bakerlite switches and one windscreen wiper. If it rained, you couldn't see a bloody thing. The color scheme was beige with a pink interior—not what you'd call a chick magnet, but I didn't care. I was king of the road. After years of riding bicycles, finally here I was with my own set of wheels.

The girl I was in love with at the time lived across the river, nine miles from Dunston. One Sunday night, I dropped her off and reversed out of the cul-de-sac where she lived. The gears jammed, leaving yours truly to reverse nine miles all the way home.

Not the best way to end a date.

The Isle of Man

ESCAPING THE TAX MAN

Paul Thompson is the drummer for Roxy Music. Paul's one of the good guys. He's a lovely Geordie boy, but getting a sentence out of him is like pulling teeth.

Paul and I lived together for a while on the Isle of Man to escape the tax man. After six weeks on the island, I ran back to the tax man and begged forgiveness. I don't care who gets upset. Don't fucking go there, unless you're a motorcycle fan or a Norman Wisdom fanatic—which I happen to be, but I *still* wouldn't go back there.

Paul's mum was great. She was one of those ladies like your aunt or grandmother, who, though not dyslexic, just got words wrong. We were once driving from Carlisle to Newcastle on the A69 (you'll notice there aren't many freeways up north), and the first leg was through dark, twisting roads, about eleven at night. Halfway there, we see the orange glow of Hexham, and she uttered the immortal words:

"Ooh, our Paul, thank Heavens we're back to civil aviation!"

Lovely!

P.S.: I'm telling you this because it happened in a car.

Reckless on the Airbus 320

"WHAT THE FUCK ARE YOU DOING?"

I was given the controls of the Airbus by an Australian pilot. "Right, Brian, take the stick and she'll just about fly herself."

We were at thirty thousand feet and approaching Sydney airport. The sun was setting and Sydney looked, well, clean, that "clean as a catwalk model's bum" sort of clean. Corrr! Er, sorry. Anyway, there I was, Brian Biggles, flying this monster.

"Okay, bring her down to twelve hundred, Mr. Johnson." I pushed the stick forward a bit and down we went. I have to admit he was doing some fancy fingerwork on knobs and switches, but all officers like myself need a batman, or engineering butler.

Oh my, there's the Opera House, looking like three seagulls eating each other, and there's the Sydney Harbour Bridge.

"Has anybody flown underneath that in one of these?" I asked.

"Yes," replied the pilot. "And they're all dead."

"Okay, a thousand feet," a recorded voice in the cabin said. "Prepare to land, fasten seatbelts, and stop shagging in the restrooms." You can't beat an Aussie airline.

"Wheels down." I was getting a little nervous. "Watch out for that side wind."

"Oh yeah, a little left rudder."

Bollocks that Sydney Harbour Bridge looked inviting, you know. I could just squeeze underneath that Tyne bridge copy if I held my nerve. C'mon, Brian, son. I moved the stick over and down we went.

"What the fuck are you doing, ya mad bastard?" the pilot said.

"I think I can do it."

"No, you fuckin' can't, you Pommie git!"

"We won the Ashes," I said. "Piss off!" I started to sweat; he started to fret. The bridge was getting closer. No way out, Brian, son, and you gotta go for it. Go, son, go! I was under! I'd done it! Then the cabin rocked violently and we hit the water. The tail had hit the bridge. The pilot looked at me and said:

"Get the fuck outta my simulator."

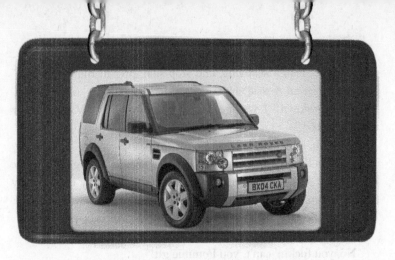

Land Rover LR3

CHEERING UP CLIFF

I bought a new Land Rover (LR3, as they're known in America) at Christmas 2005. I liked the look of it. My wife, Brenda, said it was sexy. She's American, which explains that. Anyway, we also have an aluminum Airstream, a beautiful throwback of U.S. flair. One day we heard the dreadful news that Cliff (yup, Ferrari Cliff) had got himself in a bad way. He had tripped over a log or something whilst carrying a paraffin lamp. The glass smashed, he fell on it and cut himself pretty bad. By that I mean the tendons to all his fingers were severed. Not good for one of the finest bass players in the world.

Six hours of microsurgery later, he was put back together, but he was in extreme pain, plus he didn't know whether he would play again. This happened at his summer home at Lake Toxaway, North Carolina, a gorgeous house in the Smoky Mountains. I said to Brenda, "Shit, let's go and cheer him up."

So I hooked up the Airstream to the Land Rover and off we went. Nine and a half hours later, we arrived at Wherethefuckarewe campsite, situated in a beautiful valley, accessed by a perilous downhill unpaved road. And by downhill, I mean, frikkin' steep.

There was a beautiful brook running right by the site we camped at. Cliff and Georgeanne, his wife, came to visit us, and we had prepared dinner. It started to rain, Jacques Cousteau stuff. Georgeanne took Cliff back home, before the Prozac wore off, and the brook became a river, the river became a torrent, and the torrent became an evacuation order.

The campsite owner was screaming, "Everybody leave now. The valley's flooding. Leave your vehicles and walk up the road as quick as you can!"

It was two in the morning. The water was up to the axles on the Rover and the Airstream. I jumped out of the trailer and hooked it up to the LR3, water up to my knees. Then I got in the Land Rover, started her up, and hit the magic yellow button which guarantees to pull you out of Hell if need be.

The park owner shouted, "You guys are nuts! You're never gonna make it!"

I didn't care. I just knew it would do it, and as we pulled that Airstream out, up a very steep hill, on non-tarmac breaking-away-at-the-sides road in Horrific Conditions, I started to laugh. That little bugger was doing it, nonstop, slow, sure, steady, sooo English. We will fill up our walls with our English dead, and let all those who lie abed this day think themselves accursed, for we shall cry, "Harry, England," etc., etc. Whoa, sorry, guys. Got carried away there. But I gotta tell ya, it really felt like that.

The best SUV in the world.

Road Trip

DRIVE THIS

I love to drive on "special" roads, roads that make you smile. Like the roads in the Alpine passes, the Pacific Coast Highway, the "Dragon's Tail" in North Carolina. But there are two special drives in England that get me every time. Yes, England. Where it takes five years to build five miles of motorway, where there will never be an out-of-work cone-maker, where you never see anybody actually doing anything, anytime (except at about ten at night, so they can shine those huge zillion-shagawatt lights in your eyes so you can't see what they are not doing), where motorway service stations are anything but (the food is rotten, the staff wooden, and the gas unarmed robbery).

Anyway, I digress. Take the A69 to Haydon Bridge, and just before you get there, turn left on the A686 to Alston. Then just sit back and enjoy. The scenery is great, and the road exciting enough to make you pay attention.

After about forty-five minutes, you come to Alston, the highest village in England, so I am told. Check out the cheese shop—there is some wonderful stuff in there. Cow's Udder Edam, Mrs. Thompson's Cheddar, The Woman Down the Road's Camembert. Well, not exactly, but you get my drift. Then on to Melmerby, where you've got to stop at the baker's and try the cheese scones. As my good friend Red from South Carolina would say, "They are sooo delicious they make you wanna slap yo' momma!" They are very good and as light as a butterfly's bum.

The scenery changes there, to moorland, cold and bleak, but there's more to come. You have to come back down, and that's when you think you are in Switzerland. The road zigzags all the way down to the M6, and it's steep and lots of fun. You think some guy's gonna stop you and charge you for it! Once over the M6, you shoot on to the A66 past Underskiddaw until you get to Keswick and the Lake District—which is everything you think it is going to be.

I know the M1 is not a great driving road, but it's what's at the end of it that counts for me. You see, driving up from London, Newcastle's at the end. When I see the Angel of the North (which I still think looks like a guy saying, "Honest, it was this big!"), I smile a lot. I still love driving to Newcastle. I still feel like I am driving home, even though I haven't lived there for twenty-five years.

The countryside in Durham and Northumbria still fills the eye with an unexpected beauty, and the colors of the fields at sunset make you feel poetic. But no words match, no language can re-create it, so it's best to drive and drink it in with your eyes.

To see it yourself, drive to the military road just off the A69, west of Newcastle, on the way to Hadrian's Wall. The road itself is a fabulous roller-coaster ride. That makes the car tax feel worth it. Except it was built by the Romans!

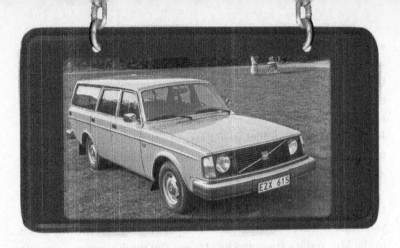

Brendan Healey

DRINKING FRACTIONALLY

Brendan Healey, who played keyboards in Lindisfarne's latter days, is one of the funniest and most brilliant musicians I have ever met. His motorcar stories are legend. You see, Brendan's modus operandi is to buy cars on the edge of extinction and drive them until they stop. He says this saves money, as there is no devaluation. Every car he buys is immediately fitted with a fundamental element that Brendan cannot do without while traveling the length and breadth of England, performing. No, not a GPS, not a hands-free phone, not a Bluetooth. It's a kettle. Yup, he likes to brew a cup of tea on the move. He says there is nothing dangerous about it: "I *have* got my seat belt on."

When his last car expired, on the M6, the AAA mechanic said, "Mr. Healey, when was the last time you put oil in this?" Brendan replied, "Where do you put that?" So now I think you are beginning to understand him . . .

I was with him once when he took his latest piece of crap to a garage-mechanic friend because the engine wasn't pulling too good. His friend pulled his head out of the engine bay and said, "Nothing wrong with it, mate. I think you're just getting too fat." Without a pause, Brendan replied, "The only reason I'm fat is because every time I shag your wife she gives me a chocolate biscuit." That one dropped me and the mechanic.

Brendan bought a Volvo. Being six foot four inches tall, he loved it, and it lasted for about four months (a keeper). But one fateful night, at the Beehive pub, the sky was as black as a hippopotamus's unwiped arse and the rain was lashing down. Brendan, refreshed after libations with fellow libationists, got into his Volvo. He roared out of the car park and into five feet of water that had gathered in a severe dip in the road. The police and fire brigade found him sitting on the top, dangling his feet through the sun roof, smoking a cigarette and soaked to the skin. He said, "Brian, if that car hadn't had a sun roof I could have drowned! Thank God I didn't have my seat belt on!"

But my favorite Brendan story is the one when he was stopped by a policeman one night.

Policeman: "Have you been drinking?"

Brendan: "Fractionally."

Policeman: "Right. Out of the car now."

Brendan poured himself out of the car, a little groggy. Just then there was an almighty bang behind the policeman. Another car had hit a lamppost.

Policeman: "Stay here, don't move—I know ya face."

After about thirty minutes, Brendan got bored and drove off. The next morning, a policeman was at his front door.

Policeman 2: "Mr. Healey, were you out driving last night?"

Brendan: "No, not me, officer."

Policeman 2: "You do have a car though?"

Brendan: "Oh yes, I do."

Policeman 2: "Where is it?"

Brendan: "It's in the garage."

Policeman 2: "Could I see it?"

Brendan: "Certainly." He opened his garage door.

Policeman: "Mr. Healey, how long have you been driving a police car?"

I'm not going to write anything more about this wonderful man, because he's got his own book to write and I want to read it first.

Crackerjack

IT ALL STARTS WITH THE TOYS

Jimmy Nail is an articulate man on subjects ranging from global warming to the vagaries of a politician's brain. Alas, this all goes down the toilet when the subject of motorcars comes up: he is a majestic car crackerjack.

"Phwoar! Look at that, man! Hey, Jonna, I'll bet that'll go some."

Yup, it's funny how we are all drawn together; like flies 'round shit, as my good friend Red from South Carolina would say. Jimmy says it's an automatic hard-on! Auto erection, and he's dead right. Hot babe—Ferrari—hot babe—Ferrari—hot babe—Ferrareeeee, and bingo! You've had an orgasm.

Jimmy, like me, was brought up on a council estate, the projects in Newcastle. He was, and still is, a big lad, "as fit as a butcher's dog," my dad would have said. He had the same dreams as me: music was the passport and playing was the visa. All he had to do was get them stamped. Jimmy raises an interesting point. "Brian, what kind of model cars did you have?"

I've forgotten all about my toys. They were all cars and airplanes, and of course my bike with a lollipop stick in the spokes to make it sound like a car (it sounded more like ten people eating spaghetti with chopsticks). Like Jimmy, and a thousand other kids, we had a Scalextric race set, and we both remember the smell of melting dynamos and oil stinking up the house. Jimmy says Hillman Imps played a big part in his life, because the police were using them as panda cars. (Only in England could we call a police car a "panda." What was that all about? Oh bugger, I'm digressing again.) How they got him into the back of one of the smallest piece-of-shit cars on the planet is a mystery of David Copperfield proportions. I had a Hillman Imp. I drove it for a week, and then it sat in my backyard for a year. My stamp collection was more useful.

Jimmy served his apprenticeship at C. A. Parsons, same as me, and had his own adventures to reach the "Toppermost of the Poppermost" (© John Lennon. Read his book!) and become very famous, but he still had to go through the group-van phase, and all that.

Now he has an Audi S8 with four hundred horses pulling him down the King's Highway. I was with him once. I swear the man whoops like a Wells Fargo stagecoach driver. When that turbo kicks in, you see he can't help it. That's why I love him. Car nut.

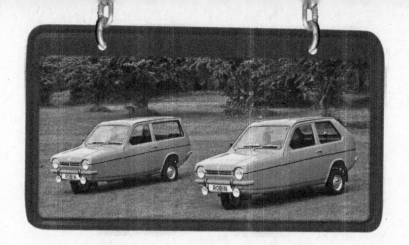

Take a Backseat

"DON'T BE SHY, YOUR MOTHER WASN'T."

In the sixties, the place to take your "lass," as we called them in Newcastle, was Tynemouth car park on the sea front. Bouncing up and down, these old (and I mean *old*) cars looked like they were making a rough Channel crossing. Seeing a female ankle in a handle strap was a sure sign someone had triumphed.

Geordie love echoed across the tarmac:

"Gerrin', you fucka."

"If you come inside of us, I'm telling my dad."

"Move over, you cow."

"I've told you before, *don't* come inside us."

If you had a Mini Cooper, you were in business. They were so convenient, you see, because they had sliding windows. A lady could position herself quite comfortably by sticking one of her legs out of the window, the other over the driver's seat, leaving me, for example, to position myself in her nether regions.

You could count on me to say something romantic. You would be surprised how many times "Don't be shy, your mother wasn't" did the trick.

One night, a girl's father came running out of his house as I was dropping her off. He wanted to know what had been going on. "Nothing" was the reply.

Then he spotted the semen on the top of her blouse. I gunned it.

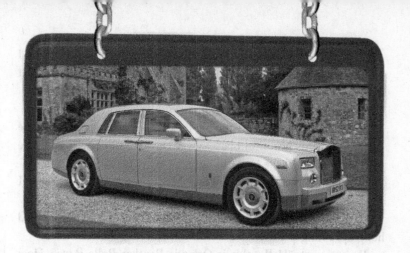

The Phantom

THE BLACK VELVET HUMPBACK WHALE

I loved my Bentley Continental. It had the look, the speed, the comfort and holy-fucking-shit acceleration. I swore it was all I ever needed.

But my good friend and snake charmer Monty Patterson, the Orlando Rolls and Bentley dealer, had other ideas. He rang me.

"Ah, Brian. I hope I find you in good favor?" I smelled a rat. "Isn't it a lovely day?"

"It is a lovely day, Monty," I said. "What's afoot?"

"How long have you had your Bentley?" he asked. Oh no, here it comes.

"Three years, Monty, and I've only got fourteen thousand miles on it. Why?"

"Oh, a magnificent motor carriage has just arrived at the dealership," Monty replied.

"Mmmmm," I said.

"Would you like to know what it is?"

"No, Monty, I wouldn't."

"Good! Well, it's a Rolls-Royce Phantom with only eight hundred miles on it, barely a year old. I sold it to a lady in Palm Beach just under a year ago and it hasn't even been farted in."

"How do you know?" I asked him.

"I've met the woman. It's too big for her. I could do a deal with the Bentley and this beautiful black velvet David of motorcars could be yours." I could feel the hook going in.

"Listen, oh rock-'n'-rolling one," Monty went on. "Why don't I send it down on the trailer and you can test-drive it?"

"No, no, Monty. Don't do that. Monty! Monty!" The bugger had hung up. I rang back.

Receptionist: "Hello, this is Orlando Bentley, Rolls-Royce. How may I direct your call?"

Me: "Monty Patterson, please."

Receptionist: "Oh, are you Mr. Johnson?"

Me: "Yes, I am."

Receptionist: "Well, he says to tell you that he's not in. Bye." Bugger. I knew the thing was already on its way. Forty-five minutes later, the doorbell rang.

"Hi, Chuck from Rolls-Royce." Now, I know it's a three-hour drive from Orlando. That meant the car had already been on the road for two hours when Monty called me. I went out to the front drive. Chuck was already opening the back door of the trailer. All I could see was this black shadowy thing the size of a humpback whale. He let it out slowly into the sunshine. It wasn't black, it was black velvet. It was stunning. I was floored. Everything started to go north on me. Nipples, willy, corners of mouth, hair . . . while the jaw went south. It was a proper Rolls-Royce. Not the 1970s–2000 ones. It was just like the ones I saw as a kid. Huge buggers.

"Here are the keys, Mr. Johnson. Take it for a spin." I got in. It was the tits. It was perfect. Lalique interior lights, suicide back doors. It was posh as fuck. My arse was going like a squirrel eating nuts. I pressed the starter button, and 2.5 tons of hand-built sex, with a 7.2 BMW engine with twelve funnels of fun took off and got me to 60 mph in about five and a bit seconds. Mine, all mine. I slobbered. I got back to my house.

"Well, Mr. Johnson, whaddya think?"

"Mine, all mine." I picked up the phone.

Receptionist: "Hello, Orlando . . ."

Me: "Get me that bugger Patterson!"

Receptionist: "Of course, sir!"

Monty: "Hey, Brian, my friend . . ."

Me: "Monty, you sneaky rotten bastard. You camel-humping four-flusher, you—"

Monty: "So you want it, don't you?"

Me: "'Course I want it." The deal was done over the phone. Chuck loaded the Bentley up. There was a tear in my eye and in my wallet when he left. But there in the driveway was my Rolls. So I wasn't going to be lying on my deathbed saying, "I wish I'd bought a Rolls." Even the great God of motorcars, *Top Gear*'s Jeremy Clarkson, said it was fab. So there you go.

I had only had the car a week when the phone call came in: "Hey, Brian, we'll need you for rehearsals in Philly next week." Bollocks! Since then I've only driven it once, and it was early 2008, and— shit!—the Black Ice tour didn't finish until August 2010. Fate can be a bit of a bastard at times.

My First Race Meet

FINDING THE AUTODROME

In a land called Dunston many years ago, three friends, Brian Johnson, George Beveridge, and Ronnie Swaddle, decided to go and watch a motor race. Now, that was like finding a bishop at a bar mitzvah in the northeast of England. After much searching, we found that there was a race at Croft Autodrome at one P.M. on Sunday. Great! It would certainly spice Sunday up. You see, I hate Sundays. It's the day before you go back to work, it's the premature end of the weekend, it's bath night, it's *Sunday Night at the Bloody London Palladium*, it's "I've set the alarm for 5:30 A.M." night. But this weekend, we were going to the races in my trusty Ford Popular.

The trouble was, I hadn't passed my driving test yet, but I was dying to drive somewhere far away. It would be an adventure. My dad was working overtime that weekend, so I could slip off my learner plates and bugger off. Croft was at least thirty-five miles away. Wow! That meant putting more than one gallon in the car. I'd never done that before, so we had a whip-round. We woke to black skies, which is normal up there in the Geordie foothills. I picked up George and Ronnie. We filled up the tank with three gallons of gas—I'd never seen a guy pump for that long. (They didn't have self-service pumps then.) The gas gauge was up to half-full—something else I'd never seen before. Right, lads, check food.

George: "I've got two teacakes with jam and a stottie cake with ham and pease pudding."

Ronnie: "I've got cheese and onion, and one and a half mince pies, because I've already eaten a bit. Oh, and a flask of tea."

This was going brilliant. I had six of my mother's famous home-made doughnuts and a couple of Spam-and-beetroot sandwiches, because my ma was Italian and couldn't quite figure out what went with what. (Rhubarb and corned beef was a particular favorite of mine.)

"Who's got the map?" I asked. The look on their faces was like one of those Japanese red-arse monkeys when they're sitting in the hot springs—or Roger Moore showing "anger" in a Bond movie. It told me we didn't have one. "It's near Middlesborough, or Darlington. Or Catterick or something," said the Swaddle. Not so brilliant. Here we were on our first real trip, with no idea how to get there. Ronnie ran back into the house and asked his dad, and came out with directions and off we went.

The names of some of the villages and hamlets we passed through are just great: Middleton Tyas, Yafforth, Snape, Kirkbymoorside, and, my personal favorite, Ainderby Quemhow. Yup, it exists. It's on the B6267, right next to Berryhills. None of them beats the daddy of them all, in Northumbria. It's called Once Brewed and it's about half a mile down the road from Twice Brewed, named by a Cromwellian general. He wanted his beer brewed twice so he moved his headquarters from Once Brewed. No, I'm not taking the piss. It's true! Christ, I'm off on a tangerine again—back to the story.

As we headed south, it started to rain, good old-fashioned sideways-windy stuff. The Ford Popular had only one windscreen wiper (the deluxe model, the Prefect, had two), which worked on a kind of vacuum power off the thingy in the carb stuff. The thing is, the more power you needed, the more you put your foot on the accelerator, the slower the wiper moved. I couldn't see much of anything. We suddenly went over a rather large bump about the size of a dinosaur's arse.

"What the hell was that?" I said.

George looked out the back window. "You've just driven over a roundabout."

Oh my God, I hadn't even seen it coming. This driving stuff wasn't as easy as I'd thought. The rain was still lashing down and we were lost—I mean "you couldn't find your dick in ten degrees below" kind of lost.

There were no signs for Croft Autodrome. No arrows to point the way. Nothing to get you there until we spotted some old hangars and drove down this old concrete road to where a soaked woman was selling tickets to get in. But there was nothing to get into, just vast swathes of grass and concrete runways. We could have driven 'round ourselves. There were no pits, just oil drums to denote the corners. This was not what we'd had in mind.

Five cars started the race, all MG TCs, and they weren't very fast or noisy. They would pass us, then we'd stand there wet and miserable for a few minutes, and then they'd pass us again. It was like watching snails shag. We decided to head for home, if we could find it, before my dad got home from work.

We got back into the "Pop" and the windows misted up. I mean, it looked like a heavy fog, and no amount of wiping did any good. "We'll have to drive with the windows open to let the air in." Well, with the wiper doing its impersonation of Errol Flynn's dick, we moved cautiously forward, my head out the window, like the pilot of a Sopwith Camel coming in to land. Shit! We'll never get home at this speed. My dad's gonna kill me if he finds out I've been out without a qualified driver in the car. My goose'll be cooked, my sausage sliced, my provisional license lost forever. We got back at seven thirty, the six-volt headlights hardly making a dent in the rain and gloom. I dropped off the lads and headed for the retribution waiting at home. When I got there, I knocked on the front door, because I still didn't have a key. My old man opened it.

"Where you been?" he asked.

I looked him in the eye and said, "I've been at George's house all day listening to music, Dad."

He looked over my shoulder at the car, which was covered in mud from the track, and said, "Did you learn ya lesson?"

I looked down and sighed. "Yes, Dad."

"Go on, get a cup of tea."

He was a cool dude.

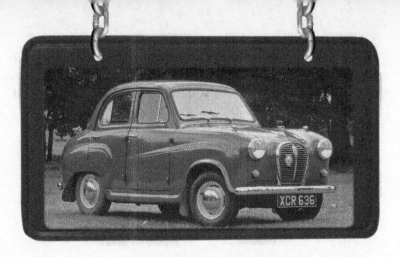

Austin A35

A SMILING PREGNANT SNAIL

Just before I joined Geordie, I bought an Austin A35, basically because it was cheap and nobody else wanted it. It was black, and the registration was POB 96. So they nicknamed me POB, in Geordie. My daughter Kala married a Geordie lad called Pob many years later. Friggin' spooky, eh?

This car resembled a pregnant snail with a smile on its face. It was tiny and powerless and a tad embarrassing to be seen in, but it had two doors, very little rust, and a real MOT. You see, MOTs were a constant source of worry to the lads I knew. Most of us had old bangers, and there was always something needed fixing to pass "the test." A tax disc fashioned out of a Brown Ale label was a good trick to keep you on the road. My insurance was on the cusp of being legal. Lenny, the insurance bloke, got me the cheapest third-party-only insurance—third party *only* if the first and second party are not in the vicinity of the accident, or the third party is the thief that pinches it. Well, I was all right there. Nobody was gonna nick this car, because they'd get caught by a policeman on foot.

The sound of the engine on this thing always amazed me. It was unique. It sounded a bit like a truffle pig eating a plate of jelly. The thing is—it kept going. And I still miss the little bugger.

I remember taking a trip to a stately home with a mate and his wife. Now, Billy's wife was a charming girl from Hartlepool who worked in a rope factory in Wallsend, but she wasn't all bad (apart from looking bored at everything around her). I mean, she never drank her pint all in one go, she always farted out loud so that you knew it was her, and she had a laugh like a hyena getting its balls chewed off by a not-very-hungry lion. She did have some culture, though I suspect that was the yogurt in the fridge. She had a beehive hairdo, which was a little out of date in 1970. She sat in the back, where the roof line was very low, and her platinum thatch now looked like it was attached to the roof. But she hadn't noticed. Should I say something? Well, Billy didn't look bothered, so I didn't. It wasn't until she got out of the car that the full damage was revealed. Her armor-like hairspray had kept everything in place, but her hive was now shaped like an Austin A35 roof lining, and she still didn't know.

I bit my lip. Billy still didn't notice, even though people were pissing themselves. At last she went to the toilet. I heard the scream. She came out, lips back in a rictus grin, eyes just slits, claws out. She shuffled penguin-like up to Billy (knickers 'round her ankles—I didn't realize she was an Elvis fan) and fetched him one right across the chops, followed by a testicular backhand that woulda done Boris Becker proud. "You friggin' bastard, I'll twat you when I get home."

The drive home was fun. Billy was getting smacked every couple of minutes: "Twat!" Then, bang!

"C'mon now, guys. Take it easy."

"And you can piss off an' all, you little twit," she said.

Finally I got them home to North Shields. She stormed out of the car and tottered on her high-heeled white kinky boots to the front door.

"Please can I come back with you?" Billy begged, and like a good friend, I said, "Piss off! She'll only come and get you again."

So Billy got out of the car, head down, knowing what he was in for. Now I knew why Billy worked more overtime that anyone else.

Fun days apart, the little car at least got me to work on time and was reliable, even though I got passed by the double-decker bus on the Coast Road.

Malcolm Young

OCCUPATION: WORLD'S GREATEST RIFFMEISTER

Malcolm Young bought a brand-new Jaguar in 1992 and didn't sell it till 2006. Okay, there's nothing wrong with that, but he didn't buy anything else, either. He doesn't really give a shit about motorcars, he's the James May of rock 'n' roll. Then again, he's had the same guitar since 1974.

He just bought a 2008 Nissan people-carrier. (I mean, what else could they carry?) He likes it a lot. I wouldn't worry so much, but this is the lad who wrote riffs like "Highway to Hell" and "Shook Me All Night Long" and loads of other great shit.

Which throws out the window all my theories about rock 'n' roll and cars. Christ on a bike, how could he do this to me?

But the Lord visited Mal the other day and He did say unto him, "Malcolm, you must go unto the light and speak with your spirit within, that spirit being Jonna."

And lo and befuckinghold, he did!

"Hey, Jonna, that Bentley Continental looks nice. I might buy one."

I looked at him like I'd just farted. He looked at me like he was just going to. My heart raced and my shoes unlaced. Was this it? The breakthrough? Mal, my Mal, was becoming a born-again motorist. I sang:

(To the tune of "Onward Christian Soldiers")
Onward Saabs and Audis,
Chryslers, Jags, and Fords,
Ferrari, Maseratis,
Morgans, Fiats, Cords,
Bentley Continental, Bee Em Double U's,
Lamborghini Muiras, Aston Martins, too.
Mal is actually thinking
Of buying a new car.
I bet my bottom dollar
It's a Jaguar.

You know, there's a song in there somewhere. Oh shit, I missed out Mercedes and a load of others.

Then Mal said, "Ah, we're too busy right now. I think I'll wait till the tour finishes in a year and a half."

Busy, too fuckin' busy! I've got to help this lad out.

P.S.: Dear Mal, I take no responsibility for what happened on this page. It was my hand what done it—Brian.

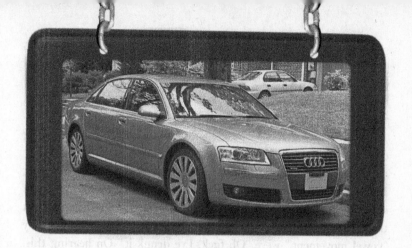

Günther

IF A MARINE WERE ON STEROIDS AND DRIVING

Although you'll have never heard of him, Günther is a very well-known driver in rock 'n' roll circles. He owns and operates the biggest tour-car company in Europe. He always has the latest Beemers, Mercs, and Audis. At first, I was the only one that would travel with him, because he was so fast, 150 mph average speed, but it didn't matter to me, he was so good. There's nothin' like havin' a glass of wine and a cheese and ham sandwich whilst going pukka-style speeds. I was later joined by that ne'er-do-well bass player of ours, Cliff Williams, who's a bit of a chicken when it comes to goin' fast. Cliff and I have traveled thousands of miles with Günther.

Günther has a German-style haircut, i.e., like a marine on steroids, a square jaw, piercing blue eyes, and he never turns 'round while he's driving, which a lot of other drivers do, scaring the shit out of you in the process. His eyes are glued to the road, while me and Cliff would be laughing and giggling in the back, the smell of the lords' lettuce wafting around him affecting him not a jot. Meanwhile, we just went faster and faster, especially on the night drives.

The new Audi RS8 was his particular favorite on the 2000 tour, and it was a great car. Unfortunately, Cliff and I were too stoned and drunk to realize, cars all seem the same when you're sitting in the back. I wonder if anyone will do a backseat-passenger car review, with all the nuances and clever clichés used in today's media.

We knew we were always safe with Günther. Even when, heading east, he had that look of a Panzer officer invading Poland.

Once, when Cliff said to me after three hours' driving, "'Ere, Jonna, I've spilled me liter bottle of Glenfiddich," we thought, "Oh shit, this car's brand-new." We got on our hands and knees and felt the carpet. It was bone-dry, and the words from Cliff, or should I say "vowel movement," were "Oh fuck, I've drunk it." On hearing this, Günther stopped the car, opened the boot, and produced another bottle. Cliff was so happy he got out of the car to have one of his five-minute roadside pees, which is hilarious, because he tends to shrug his shoulders a lot and talks to his dick, and when he's finished, he doesn't so much shake as wrestle the thing back into his pants.

That night ended fabulously when we arrived in a French town, at about four thirty in the morning. A crowd of about two hundred kids was waiting for us. Günther opened the door and we spilled out the same door, giggling and laughing, onto the road. The crowd went crazy—this was just what was expected.

That's when Günther had just told us the only joke he could remember. He said you must always remember: the bigger the German, the smaller the swimsuit. I still laugh at it.

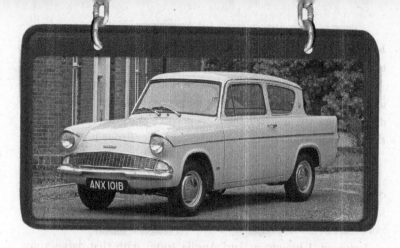

My Brother, Maurice

CAR RATS IN ARMS

Maurice was the brother with the name my mother wanted. "Maurice Chevalier was so 'andsome," she would say in her lovely Italian accent. Maurice was the first in the family to "go on the road." He was a car rat as well; he still is mentally retarded, in an "I don't know what to buy next" way. He lives happily in Whickham, with his two children, a Porsche convertible, and a 1965 Karmann Ghia—I think one of the prettiest little VWs. His two human children, Mark and Michael, are helplessly like their dad and uncle: car crazy. They say we don't have branches on our family tree, just wing mirrors. When we gather at pubs, we tend to look more like an assembly line than a family.

Back in '65, Maurice was the first one to be able to buy something new, a Lambretta scooter. He was a bellboy at the County Hotel in Newcastle. He was apprenticed to become a bellman. Tips flowed in, and he poured them into his piggy bank. After about six months, he was off—he'd heard there were rich pickings to be had bellboying in

Jersey. I missed him. He was my younger brother; there was nothing to kick (the cat had left months ago).

He returned a year and a half later. And outside was parked a Triumph Spitfire hardtop, white and gorgeous. It was his. Maurice was dressed smartly and had them proper driving gloves on, the kind that look like someone's just knitted the back of your hand.

"Wanna come for a drive?"

"Oh yeah!" I said. That's hard to say with your tongue hanging out. It was a beautiful little car—until some little shit scratched it or kicked one of the panels in a fit of envy. You had to be careful in the northeast in those days.

Later on, I bought a Ford Anglia 100E, with that daft wrong-way-'round back screen. Maurice had moved back to Newcastle and was courting.

"A woman," he told me.

He sold the Spitfire for a profit and he bought my Anglia. Now this car went from 0 to 60 mph in the time it takes to spit-roast a fair-size bullock. That didn't faze my bro. If it wasn't fast, he'd make it look like it was fast. Money no object. He went out and bought a tin of matte-black paint and some yellow electrician's tape. Oh yeah, and a paintbrush.

But he didn't actually prepare the car, he just painted over the top of the blue bodywork (some of it missing, I may add—these were the days of the great rust epidemics that swept the length and breadth of Britain). He had that maniacal Johnson look in his eye. He was creating something beautiful. It was a masterpiece. Why was he lucky to be the only person in the world to think of it?

"Wait for the paint to dry? Wait for the paint to dry?! That's for suckers, that's for people with too much time on their hands. This is the sixties: peace, love, and shagging." (Well, once you got out of Gateshead.) "This car's going to be Psychedelic Moody Maurice's Manwagon." Oh shit. While he's up there talking to Zeus and the other lads up there, asking for tips, his friend Dennis arrives. Dennis is an apprentice plasterer and perfect for the job of helping Maurice put on the stripes.

Dennis always looked a happy man, mainly because his teeth were too big for his mouth, or perhaps because he'd just come from the pub. There they were, Maurice at the front, Dennis at the back.

"Right, Dennis, I'm pulling back the tape now . . . Dennis, Dennis, where the frig are you?"

"I'm here, but I can't hear you for the traffic."

(They were doing this on the street and quite a crowd had gathered—there wasn't much telly then.) Ah yes, the tape. At last they cotton on to the fact that they're both doing the same job. They pull; they tease; the language was a pretty color purple.

"Done!" went the cry. We stood back to look. Hmm!

"Your line's not straight, mate," said Maurice.

"Looks straight to me," Dennis said.

What they'd tried to do was make it look like a race car with two stripes down the hood, over the roof, and down the boot. Electrician's tape is known for being bendy, and if you pull it, it gets skinnier and doesn't stick very well. It looked what it was: an absolute cock-up.

"Ah fuck it," Maurice said. "C'mon, Dennis, I'll drive you to the pub."

Dennis: "I'm not going in that piece of shit!"

What happened next is legend in Dunston. Dennis did get in the car, and Maurice got in, feeling pretty down. His grand plan had failed. He was as low as a lollipop lady's libido. He started the car, put it into first gear, and drove off. Then his head disappeared, the car swerved and came to a sudden stop. I ran over.

"What the hell?"

There was Maurice, still sitting in his seat. The seat was sitting on the road. The great rust epidemic had claimed another victim in Newcastle. But although the floor had fallen out of Maurice's cars, his life was pretty solid.

Angus Young

OCCUPATION: DEVILISH IMP SCHOOLBOY GUITARIST

My workmate Angus smokes tabs and drinks tea, lots and lots of both, so he is usually double-fisted when you are talking to him. He can pick up a guitar, play it, and turn it into a threatening series of events in moments.

He's quite a remarkable man, but he has a skeleton in his cupboard. And I, Brian Johnson, am about to commit the ultimate in treachery. But wait—I am no Judas! I am a good lad. So why do I have to tell you this?

My body is a cacophony of chaos.

My soul says shout about it.

My heart says howl it.

My scrotum says scroat it.

My inner being is torn between telling the truth and letting it go. But I am a gearhead, a maniacal, mechanically maladjusted fanatic. I could sell my story to *Hello!* or *OK!* or any other useless piece-of-shit magazine and become a paparazillionaire—but I can't do that. So I will tell you instead.

ANGUS DOESN'T HAVE A DRIVING LICENSE. I mean, that's like being an atheist or something, isn't it?

There, I've said it and got it off my chest.

Well, so much for Angus and cars.

Cars and Music

YOU CAN'T HAVE ONE WITHOUT THE OTHER

Rock 'n' rollers have been writing about cars since cars started looking like rock 'n' roll. Ike Turner, in between going ten rounds with Tina every night, wrote "Rocket 88" about an Oldsmobile Rocket V8. And how about "Little Deuce Coupe" by the Beach Boys?

Just a little Deuce Coupe with a flathead mill
But she'll walk a Thunderbird like it's standing still.

Jeez. I don't know whether to sing it or build it.

Then there's Chuck Berry. In between looking through peepholes into his guest bathrooms and going to jail, he wrote some crackers: "No Particular Place to Go," "Route 66." I remember Geordie supported Chuck for a week of gigs in Germany in 1975. He used all of our equipment and we didn't charge him a penny. After the last gig, he was sitting in his car, and I said, "'Scuse me, Mr. Berry, can I have your autograph?" He said, "I only sign one a day and I've already done it." Then he said, "You're from Scotland." I told him I was

English, and then he said, "You are what I say you are." It was then I told him to piss off in Scottish, English, and a Cornwall accent, just for the fuck of it. Oh yeah, and I told him he was a cunt.

The Beatles' "Baby, You Can Drive My Car" was another cracker. And how about Flanders and Swann's "Transport of Delight," that song about London buses: "The big six-wheeler, scarlet-painted, London Transport, diesel-engined, ninety-seven-horsepower omnibus." Well, it's not exactly rock 'n' roll, but it's clever. "Prince," who shall not be called an artist unless he's not called Prince, wrote "Little Red Corvette" in the eighties, and Bruce Springsteen's "Pink Cadillac" is another great one. The New Romantics had Gary Numan's "Cars." To be honest, there're so many great car songs that I could actually write a separate book about them.

What is it about cars that makes you want to write songs about them? I guess women and cars get mixed up in your head. They're sexy, they're expensive, they carry luggage and big headlights, and they're sometimes a little loose. I mean, when I wrote: "She was a fast machine / She kept her motor clean / She was the best damn woman that I ever seen," for "Shook Me All Night Long," I thought it was perfectly natural, and, thankfully, so did everyone else. So, there's the recipe: cars + women + rock 'n' roll = great songs.

Tour Bus Tippy-Toe

TAKING ON THE MENTALLY CHALLENGED
MORAL MINORITY

In the mid-'80s, the right-wing Christian Moral Majority (who are indeed a minority) decided they'd had enough. Rock 'n' roll was from Satan and they were gonna wipe it out, all songs with unseemly lyrics, i.e., "Highway to Hell," were to be banished forever, no more would there be rock concerts—which were the real cause of their kids going off the rails, it was our fault, all of it. Of course, American parents blamed rock music in the fifties, and Elvis was indeed a Satan Singer, and then, when our lord of Lennon said the Beatles were bigger than Jesus, they burned Beatles' albums, just like the Nazis burned books in Germany, now you must remember this is America we're talking about, not some far-off European Backwater. Frank Zappa went to Congress to plead our case and he came away "looking more like Jesus than anyone," knowing no one listened to a word he said.

Well, in the middle of this, we, AC/DC, were heading to Springfield, to play the arena. On the way there, Big John, our security man, said, "Listen up, lads. We've got reports that a couple of guys out there are gonna shoot at the bus."

Me: "Are you fucking kidding?"

Him: "Wish I was, but they're religious fanatics."

Holy shit, he wasn't kidding. These guys were the forerunners of the Taliban.

Me: "I think we should bravely turn around and bugger off."

Mal and Angus: "No, we can't let them beat us. We gotta do the show for the kids who bought the tickets."

Me: "But I don't wanna die in a tour bus, of bullet wounds."

Big John: "Well, why don't we all lie on the floor?" Thoughts of Clint Eastwood in *The Gauntlet* came to mind.

The driver said, "I got an idea, why don't I scroll the name signs on the front of the bus? I think there's a one saying 'Young Singers of Jesus.'" We stopped the bus and he jiggled the levers, and lo we became singers for the Lord.

(We still crouched behind the seats.)

We had also learned that the arena had been ringed by the aforementioned Mentally Challenged Minority, all holding hands and chanting in "tongues," which, translated into English, means "Bullshit." I mean, do these people actually think that we think they think they actually know what they think they're talking about? Anyway, the chorus sounded shit, because nobody knew the same words in Tongues.

The ringleader of this messy band of malcontents was none other than the She God Tipper Gore, Wife of Al, Mother of All. She wanted us banned, but more worryingly, she wanted Angus arrested for lewd behavior, because Angus always dropped his shorts and showed his bum to the audience for a split second. So, with her political clout, she had police officers placed in the audience, ready to arrest Angus the minute he displayed his ass.

We managed to get through the cordon by a rear loading bay, and our first decision was to really spoil the Tipper's night by simply not dropping said shorts. I couldn't get this thing out of my mind. I had to see what was happening, so I slipped out the back door and went to see the action in the flesh, so to speak.

I went up to some of the women standing near Tipper Gore, and they said, "Join us. We are going to stop the Anti-Christ Devil Children from performing." They meant AC/DC. Jeez, even I couldn't have thought of that one. What would my mom think of her Brian, an ex–choir boy, being called Anti-Christ? Of course, I've never been a fan of any religion; as far as I'm concerned, it was all started by two hippies and a snake, but that Jesus fella always sounded cool, and would probably have come to the show.

Tipper the Family Woman is now getting divorced, and her kids, it seems, never followed her advice, and Al's well out of it. To the people of Springfield, thanks for a brilliant show and a great night. To Tipper Gore: Don't throw stones.

Marital Blues 1968

RIDING SHOTGUN

The shotgun wounds were healing nicely. Yes, it was that kind of marriage. It is no wonder that those years are remembered by cars, not moments.

We went to Durham on honeymoon, two nights in the wife's uncle's three-bed semi, in a used Cortina Mk1 with a dodgy powder-blue paint job. It bubbled in ten days.

I was driving the same car bought on HP on a windy Sunday afternoon in North Shields (not a nice place to be) when the hood flew off. It sailed up into the air in slow motion and floated down again, nice and gentle, like a gossamer wing. I got out to pick it up. But as I reached it, the wind picked it up and blew the bastard down the road, scraping the shit out of it.

It's funny how when you have no money you have no luck with cars.

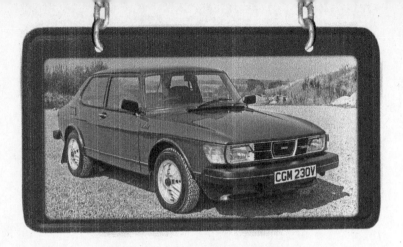

Jerry Wexler
(Rock in Peace)

RHYTHM AND BLUES AND SAABS

Jerry Wexler is probably the greatest music man of the last century. It was he, with his partner, Ahmet Ertegun, who signed Ray Charles, Sam & Dave, Aretha Franklin, Wilson Pickett, and so many others to Atlantic Records. He was the man who coined the phrase "rhythm and blues." And he was the man who took Dusty Springfield to Memphis, to produce the best album she ever made. Oh, and loads of other good shit.

He was also my mate. I met him in 1992 in Sarasota, Florida, where we both live. So why, oh why, did he drive that same old blue Saab? You see, I don't understand Saabs. They're a bit like U2: you know they're good but you just don't get it. And if you have a lisp, you can't even buy one.

I phoned Jerry in the summer of 2008.

"Hey, Jerry, it's Brian here. I'm off to England for four days to shoot a video ['Rock 'n' Roll Train,' for those among you with an interest in these things]. When I'm back, I'll come see ya."

Jerry had been very ill. He was ninety-one years old, but he was the most lucid and brilliant man I'd ever met. His stories were legend—read his book *Rhythm and the Blues*.

And even in his final days, the man had brass. He told me about being driven home one day, after one of his many visits to the hospital, by a very attractive young lady with beautiful breasts. He was curled up in the passenger seat and she asked him, "Tell me if there's anything you need, Jerry."

He said, "Oh yeah! Just let me feel one of those titties."

After the initial shock, she said, "Well, okay."

She actually got one out, and Jerry paused, looking at her.

"Shit," said Jerry. "I don't even have the strength to reach out and touch it."

True story.

Now, back to our call. "Brian," he said. "I'm checking out, kid, I've had enough. I got tubes up my ass, up my nose, in my arms. I can't taste my wine and I'm being fed through a fucking tube. It ain't living, man, do ya dig it? I'm checking out."

"Oh, shit, Jerry, don't talk like that. Hang in there."

"There's nothing to hang on with. Stay cool, kid. I'll see you on the other side."

The phone went dead and so did I. Jerry took two more days.

See ya, Jerry.

Love, Brian.

P.S.: I don't know where the Saab is. He probably left it to someone he didn't like.

Tour Bus II

"NO SHITTING ALLOWED. SHAGGING EXPECTED."

Cliff Williams was sleeping in the bunk above me on the bus one night. I was reading my book, because I'd seen all the fucking DVDs, when suddenly Cliff came flying past me and hit the floor with a tremendous thud. He also hit the air-conditioning grating, which was built into the floor. I shouted, "Wow, mate, are you okay?" Nothing. "Mate, Cliff, are you fucking alive?" Nothing. Holy shit, Cliff's dead by falling out of his bunk—this ain't gonna look good in the annals of rock 'n' roll history.

Then I heard him snoring. The fucker had fallen six feet onto his face and never even changed beat. I was very worried, so worried that I fell asleep, too. In the morning, Cliff woke with a huge bruise on his cheek the size of a good-size plum and the shape of a good-size air-conditioning unit. He looked at me seriously and said, "Hey, Jonna, did you punch me while I was asleep last night?" That's why I love Cliff.

One of the more subtle differences between American and European buses is the toilets. You can't snap one off in either, but in America, the signs on the door read: PLEASE NO SOLIDS. On one English tour bus, the sign read: NO SHITTING ALLOWED. SHAGGING EXPECTED.

"Shagging Expected," though. Usually, the back lounge in any tour bus is the scene of serious shagfests. Whatever Caligula and the inhabitants of Sodom and Gomorrah got up to, they were amateurs in comparison to what went on in these highly charged orgies, usually orchestrated by very experienced road crew. The smell of the Lord's lettuce hangs like a shroud over the contestants in the Last Willy Standing competition, usually about five in the morning. The trouble is nobody remembers much about it the next day. It's a pisser all those great times go unremembered.

Sad to say, after the great AIDS scare back in the eighties, things changed. There was terror in the eyes of the road crew and band members; those who still had members were very grateful.

The Things You Do for Vans

PARACHUTE JUMPING AIN'T FUN

It was around 1968. I was newly married, with a daughter (Joanne); I wanted transport badly, but I also needed a PA system so I could continue singing in bands. My wages from C. A. Parsons, where I was working as an apprentice, were, to put it mildly, useless. What to do? Who to turn to? My dad had nothing to spare, and my wife's dad didn't care. Then I saw it, a recruiting poster for the Territorial Army Parachute Regiment, monthly pay and extra for every jump you did, eight whole pounds extra. I was only getting five pounds a week at Parsons, and all I had to do was jump out of airplanes as a part-time job. Okay, there was the danger of falling two thousand feet and getting light bruising, but the money, son, the money.

I signed up, then had to go straight to parachute school. Anyway, I thought I could now buy a second- or thirdhand car. North Shields is a good place to come from, and that's where I lived. With my own wheels, I could leave anytime, and I wanted to so badly. The money from two weeks of bloody scary Cold War exercising in Germany helped me buy a secondhand PA system with two four-by-eight speakers and a hundred-watt WEM amp. Oh boy, now the only trouble was I was so busy at work and in the TA and at technical college (for I would be a draftsman—a rotten one, I'll admit, but I was one once).

Automobiles in the shape of vans became my focus. Cars were for normal people; us musos wanted vans. Of course, Ford Transits were quite new—the Beatles and the Stones had them. I'm afraid our vans were more agricultural, clapped-out Ford Thames/Commer crap. My very first van was a Hillman Husky, a legend in van culture. All Hillmans rusted before you got them home from the showroom, and this one was ten years old! I did have a brake-light guarantee from the used-car bloke. Once you hit the brakes and turned the corner, it was over.

When I was in a band called Fresh, we had a Commer incident. We were driving to some village near Newcastle one Saturday night. We were gonna play a gig to the yokels, and the tottie was supposed to be hot. On the way, the whole back floor of the Commer collapsed, just went down, and there were the back tires, bald, of course, spinning 'round, and our gear starting to fall out the back. We stopped as quickly as our brakes—and I use the term loosely—could stop us. We were fucked. I can't remember how we got back.

Car Porn

MAKE SURE THE DOOR'S LOCKED

To show you what man can do with metal, I give you the beauty of:

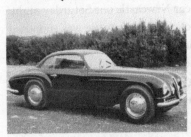

1942 Alfa Romeo 6C 2500 Tipo Sport

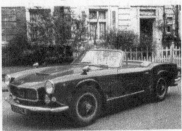

1963 Maserati Vignale Spyder

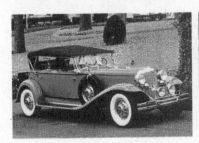

Chrysler Duel Cowl Phaeton

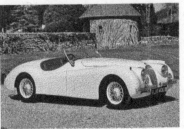

Jaguar XK 120

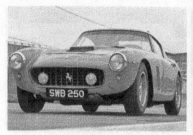

1962 Ferrari 250 SWB

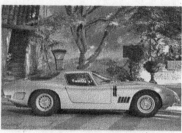

Bizzarrini 5300 GT Strada

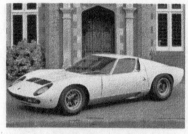

Lamborghini Muira

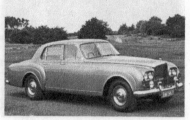

1960s Bentley Continental Flying Spur

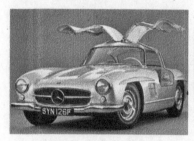

Mercedes 300SL Gullwing

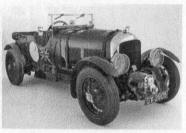

Bentley racer, 4.5 litre, supercharged

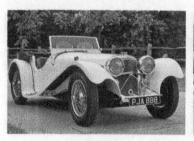

Jaguar SS100

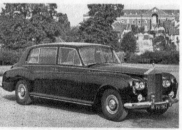

1960s Rolls-Royce Phantom

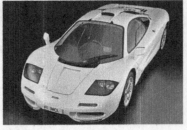

McLaren F1 . . .

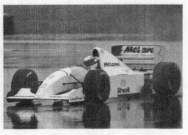

. . . and any McLaren race car

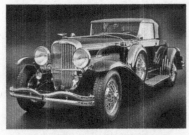

Duesenberg SJ Lagrange Phaeton

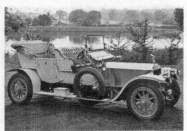

Rolls-Royce Silver Ghost

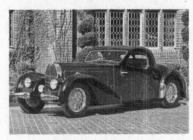

Bugatti Type 57 Atalante

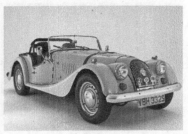

Morgan

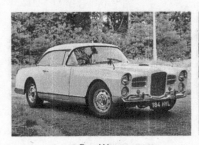

Facel Vega

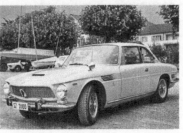

ISO Rivolta

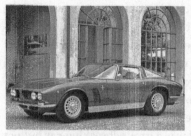

ISO Grifo

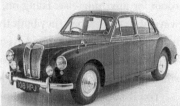

MG MPB Magnettes

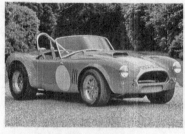

Shelby AC Cobra

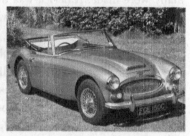

The big Austin Healey

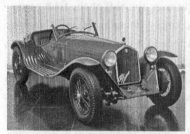

Alfa Romeo 8c Scuderia 193

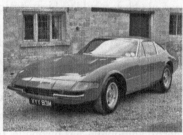

Ferrari Daytona

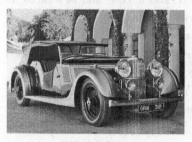

1930s Alvis Tourer

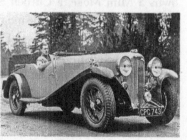

Lagonda M45

There are a lot more photos I could put in, but there wouldn't be room for anything else. Hang on, that's not a bad idea. Beauty has always been there when they built these, practicality maybe came second in the thirties and forties, and even up to the seventies. Now the Ferrari 430 is as reliable as an Audi or Toyota. The Audi R8 is a luscious, lip-smacking, liberational libation of loveliness. That's why I bought one!

You'll notice there are a couple of American cars there, the Duesenberg and the Cobra. The Cord was a groundbreaking car but not many were made. America was taken over by bean counters, those horrible, faceless little bastards with glasses perched on their noses the size of a garden gnome's dick. You won't need this; that's too expensive. Sack three hundred people and the profit goes up. Don't let management have prostitutes; tell them to have a quick one off the wrist. These useless twits were responsible for some of the most dangerous cars in the world. Remember all those Dirty Harry movies in the seventies, where shit-box Dodges and Pontiacs chased Mercs and BMWs 'round mountain roads? The way they handled, the American plodders would've been straight over the cliff at the first turn.

Anyway, it's sad. America's a country of car nuts, and they love their hot rods and their V8s, and there's racing on every weekend, racing of all kinds.

Guys like Walt Bohren. He was an IMSA national champion in the early eighties. I've codriven with him many times and he basically taught me everything I know about racing cars. He is a wonderful anglophile, a francophile. He races airplanes and motorcycles, owns a Mini Moke, a Citroën SM, and a 2CV, and he's raced an Aston Martin prototype. He mourns the passing of American muscle but believes the new Callaway Fords are the real deal. He now lives on a huge catamaran in the British Virgin Islands (oh yeah, and I visit him at every opportunity).

The thing is, I don't want the Yanks to lose what we lost, our national identity. Because that's what our cars were, for better or worse.

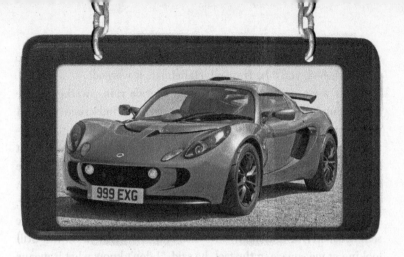

Lots of Trouble, Usually Serious

WHAT L-O-T-U-S REALLY STANDS FOR

Times move on, and in 2007 I bought a brand-new, British-racing-green Lotus Exige S. Nought to sixty in a vinegar stroke. What a gorgeous-looking car! I had a stage-two exhaust fitted so's I couldn't hear anything. The noise, oh that noise, it was absolutely fabulous! Heads turned and jaws dropped as I drove by.

Now, here's where the problem was. On the second day, my inside door handle came off in my hand. The dealership took it away; it came back four days later: "All fixed, Brian, no more problems." "Hold on," I said. "Don't leave till I try it." So I got in, tried it once, tried it twice, oh, fuck me, it's off again. The car goes back on the truck for a replacement door, and ten days later it's back. Now I'm a little suspicious of everything. And, you see, the door handle on this car is important, because the outside one doesn't really exist and the side window's too small for you to reach back and hit the button. So if you crashed, you'd be trapped. Hallelujah, it worked!

Off I went, and it started raining, Florida rain, swathes of the stuff comin' at you. I turned on the one big windscreen wiper. I want you now to imagine a noise like Mariah Carey singing full-throat with a prize leek up her arse. I nearly shat; I thought the cat had got into the engine bay. When I stopped gasping "What the fuck was that?," off it went again to the dealership. Five days later, it came back. The guy looked me straight in the feet and said, "Hey, Mr. Johnson, the destrangulation millipod was congratulating the semihydrosternic anticular." I nodded and said, "Did ya fix it?" Still looking at me square in the feet, he said, "I don't know what it means either, but the wiper's working again." Right then, I'd had this car three and a half weeks and I'd got forty-five miles on the clock.

Off we go again. My wife, Brenda, said, "Let's go for dinner in it," which was strange, because getting in and out of the bugger you had to have the moves of a young Olga Korbut. "Okay, let's go!" I was driving into town when a police car stopped me. My old mate Officer Dee. "Hey, Brian, do you know you have a brake light out?" "I can't have, me darlin', the car's brand-new." She put her foot on the brake, and she was right. I couldn't believe it! She said, "Get it fixed tomorrow. You know it's the death penalty in Florida." Funny, very funny. This was just getting worse—what else could go wrong?

Folks, get this. I drive on and come to a stop at the traffic lights in downtown Sarasota, then the right-hand headlight fell out. I mean, it popped out, it was just hanging by the wires—much to the amusement of everyone watching. Officer Dee, who was behind me, got out of her car and said, "Did you build this yourself?" That was it. I just started laughing along with everyone else.

The Lotus dealership said they were sorry, but a few other Exiges' headlights had been popping out. "Oh, well, that's all right then." They sent their top man to Tampa to go over the whole car, and I got a nine-page report on the things that hadn't even gone wrong yet. This time it was gone for two weeks—one last chance, I thought.

After two weeks, the telephone rang. It was my buddy Nick Harris, who was with the Minardi race team at Sebring. "Hey, Brian, come over. We're testing our new cars." Great, because it's a fantastic drive to Sebring from my house, State Road 71 then on to Route 66. It was 99 degrees outside. I was enjoying the drive, with the air-conditioning on full blast. Then, twenty miles from the track, it packed up. It was getting hot, and I was leaking like a pirate's poxed-up dick. God, it was hot. I made it to the track, and the Minardi guys checked over the car, said the cabin was 125 degrees.

Brilliant. How was I gonna get home and not die? I remembered *Ice Cold in Alex*, the British war movie where they started killing each other because they were, yeah, sweating. Christ, I might kill myself with the sweating thing. Calm down, lad, easy. I said my good-byes to the lads after an hour and gritted my teeth. "C'mon, you can do it."

I was driving into the sun; I had to get out two or three times to cool down in the 97 degrees outside. I got home and never put a foot in the car again. After much humming and buck-passing, I eventually got my money back, less the $12,000 the government took for tax. Governments are funny like that; once you give them money, they never wanna give it back. I told my old friend Red the story, and he said, "Braaaan, in South Carolina they say Lotus stands for Lots Of Trouble, Usually Serious." He wasn't fuckin' kidding.

P.S.: Lotus America said, "We'll give you your money back as long as you don't tell anybody about this." Since when was telling the truth illegal?

P.P.S.: Lotus, would you please tell your blind, deaf, and dumb quality-control fella to get a grip, but not on anything on a Lotus—it'll come away in his hand.

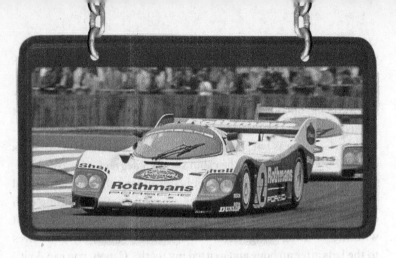

Paul Newman

GENTLEMAN OF THE TRACK

The rock 'n' roll fraternity is a strange and very close one, apart from the fact that no one talks to each other—unless Bobby Geldof and Bono have a charity bash, where everybody revels in their own self-righteous glory. (Oooh, I'm glad I got that off my chest.)

My bandmates, obviously, and the people I know in rock 'n' roll and music in general, are, I'm proud to say, good guys. Jimmy Nail is as hard as his surname but a pussycat underneath. (For God's sake, don't tell him I said that, or he'll knock the living shit out of me.)

Mark Knopfler; Tony Joe White; Donald "Duck" Dunn, the greatest bass player that lives, from Booker T and the MGs. Also he played on "Midnight Hour," "Knock On Wood," "Sittin' on the Dock of the Bay," and a shitload of other good stuff. "Green Onions," "Time Is Tight"—check these out yourself. Scotty Hill from Skid Row, Robin Zander from Cheap Trick, Billy Joel from Billy Joel, Jesse James Dupree from Jackyl, Joe Lynn Turner, Gary Numan—a great race driver and, believe it or not, a very entertaining and funny guy. It's been a pleasure and a privilege to know them all.

But one man I've had the honor to meet had nothing to do with music at all. But he *was* a racer. And he passed away three days before I wrote this very sentence.

I met Paul Newman about three times in drivers' meetings and on the track, but I never bothered him, because I knew he didn't like the fuss. A bit like myself, he thought racing was racing. The autograph and photograph stuff was taboo.

In 2000, I was recording in Vancouver, and the Grand Prix was on one weekend. I was invited to join the Newman/Haas team. That Sunday, it was black skies, then sunshine, then showtime. The race started. I was in the hot pit. Roberto Moreno was driving, and no one knew what tires to put on, wet or dry, because the weather was changing all the time. Paul "Handsome as Fuck" Newman was standing there next to little Geordie me. He turned to me after about thirty minutes and he said, "Well, what do you think, wet or dry?" I looked straight into his piercing laser-blue yaks and said, "You know, I don't work for you." He looked at me again and said, "Are you sure?" I told him who I was. "Yeah, I heard of you." Lying bugger.

In 1992, I was at the Cleveland Grand Prix in the celebrity race. It was there I met Mario Andretti, lovely man. I told him I'd love to take up race driving but thought I was too old. "No way," he said. "I taught Paul Newman when he was forty-four."

Forward to Daytona 2000. I was driving a Mazda rotary race car, and I had Paul Newman right up my arse in a 962 Porsche—as everyone knows, the "wanna fuck you" of racing cars. He was catching me, of course—he had a bigger engine—and we were going into turn two on the banking when my engine let go. It was a Jeremy Clarkson of a blowout. I slowed from about 170 mph down to 90, and I was expecting to receive a Newman enema, but he was so quick with his reactions that he drove around me. I wasn't hurt, and I knew then and there he was a great race driver. This guy raced cars, smoked tabs, and drank beer—perfect.

He was one of the most decent human beings I have ever met.

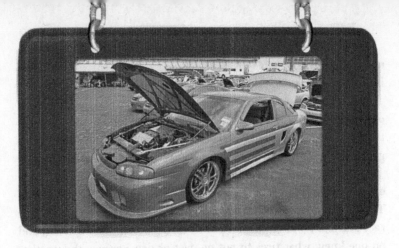

Pimp My Ride Rant

MAKING BEAUTIFUL CARS AWFUL

Janis Joplin, the most fucked-up, drugged-up, and propped-up female singer of the sixties, famously wondered in song why the good Lord wouldn't buy her a Mercedes-Benz. I am so happy she never actually drove one whilst I or any of my family members were around.

Today I live in America and I see *Pimp My Ride* cars driven by rap stars and I just laugh. What on earth makes them think they can out-think a BMW, Bentley, Mercedes, or Porsche car designer? But these buggers have chorus lines like "I shot my granny in the temple, not *inside* the temple but *in* the *temple*, shit, you know, the one on the side of the head, on the side of the road." And some of their chromium penis extensions are majestically awful; some of the wheel rims look like they've been designed by Ray Charles or George Dubya Bush's geography teacher. The gold-toothed, sixteen-charm-wearing, diamond-through-the-nose cretins who drive these cars designed for aristocraps make a regular guy wanna cry. These are the cars that should be keyed or used in a ram raid, preferably with the owners strapped to the front. These are the cars that should be stolen without delay, and shipped to Russia or China or Romania, anyfuckingwhere but near me! These cars make my arse feel like a breakaway republic, and that's not pleasant.

Woah, Brian, son, steady, take a deep breath. Shhhh, there, there. Phew, that was a close one, I nearly lost it there . . .

Awesome Bill from Dawsonville

HOW MOONSHINE MADE RACE CARS

A couple of months back, I was racing at Road Atlanta. It was the "Walter Mitty" race week, a brilliant gathering of vintage race cars. I also had to do a documentary of me driving my favorite car 'round the roads of Georgia, the car being the Rolls-Royce Phantom. So, bright and early Monday morning, the producer said, "We're going to a place called Dawsonville."

"Never heard of it," I said.

"It's basically where NASCAR had its origins," he said.

Now, Europeans usually get a little snotty when NASCAR is mentioned, because they just go "'round and 'round."

Well, I'm here to tell you that I drove one of those big buggers 'round and 'round Indianapolis Raceway, and my admiration for those boys knows no bounds, those guys go fast.

Anyhow, I arrived in Dawsonville, pulled up to the Georgia Racing Hall of Fame, and met a wonderful gentleman called Gordon Pirkle, who was the curator. Now, apart from all the fabulous cars in there, there was a moonshine still, right in the middle of the hall. Hmmm! Strange, I thought. "What's that thing for?" I asked.

"Well," Gordon said, "the first illegal liquor runners drove from Dawsonville to Atlanta fifty miles away, at night with no headlights." (They couldn't use the headlights because the revenue men were after them.)

"How did they do that?" I said.

"Well, they had to follow the telegraph poles, but only when the moon shone, 'cause you couldn't see them otherwise." Ah-ha!

"Moonshine." I suddenly got it.

When I asked Gordon if he ever ran moonshine, he said with a twinkle in his eye, "Oh yeah." And through those eyes, I saw a young man and a dusty road, driving the bejesus out of a V8 souped-up Ford on a moonlit night with no headlights and lots of balls following those telegraph poles fifty miles to Atlanta on Thunder Road. Well, people being people, they started to bet on who was the fastest driver, Gordon said. "If you came first you won, if you came second you went to jail."

So, in a strange kinda way, that's how the competitive edge came into it.

Gordon asked me if I wanted some lunch, and he happened to run a great little restaurant that served something called a Bully Burger. I asked him what was in it; he said with an extra twinkle in his eye, "Oh varmints and such." Being English, I thought it was the size of Oprah Winfrey's wallet and the best varmint sandwich I'd ever tasted. I also had some "white lightnin'," and found after drinking it that Chinese arithmetic ain't that hard.

Then the "King of kings" arrived, Bill Elliot, the winningest driver in NASCAR in his time, and born and bred in Dawsonville, hence his nickname, "Awesome Bill from Dawsonville." After five minutes with this man, you honestly think you've known him all your life; in fact, the whole town's like that, the accent is perfect, just what you want to hear in Georgia, a soft, rolling vowel movement that sounds like a warm blanket.

He took me to his race shop, and I asked him if I could have a job, he just laughed, but I was serious about it. There are two of these beasts just sitting there like greyhounds with the hare running, and them being tied up at the starting line, these cars just don't look right unless they're racing.

It was all too brief; I had to leave, and I didn't want to. It was a strange feeling: four hours ago I'd never heard of it, and now I'll probably go back every year. It's not the Pyramids, it's not the Vatican or the Sydney Opera House, but it is Gearhead Heaven. Go see for yourself.

The Greats

ARE THEY DRIVERS OR GODS?

I don't think anyone who lived through the fifties or sixties can forget the names Juan Manuel Fangio, Stirling Moss, or Jim Clark. There were lots of other great drivers: Jack Brabham, Bruce McLaren, Dan Gurney . . . I could go on. But, being English, you just loved Stirling Moss. What a name! Can you imagine at the baptism: "I name this child Stirling"? His dad had to be a money-mad banker, and the surname—Moss, a rolling stone gathers no and all that. Great stuff. It's up there with Baron von Richthofen, and he wasn't even a baron. My name's Brian Johnson, but when I'm racing I call myself Giancarlo Ferrari.

Who could forget Stirling Moss and "Jenks" driving the Mille Miglia and winning by hours? One of the great drives in mankind's history. Denis "Jenks" Jenkinson had written down the route on a kind of toilet roll and basically invented the rally system of racing. Turn one hundred yards, bend at six, over slight hill at four, I need to piss at once. But there was no stopping except for gas, and that beautiful Mercedes 300 SLR ran perfectly all day. The record still stands: How cool is that? When coppers stopped drivers in England for speeding, they would say, "I say, I say, I say. Who do you think you are, Stirling bleeding Moss?"

Juan Manuel Fangio was the granddaddy of them all. He wasn't thin, he didn't look fit, and he was in his forties when he won his fourth world championship. He wore a bloody T-shirt and loafers when he raced. His face and the faces of other racers had that great look when they took their goggles off: their eyes made them look like a panda getting shagged by an elephant. He was the greatest race driver ever, in tough competition: Tazio Nuvolari was also great, along with Ayrton Senna, Schumacher—oh, it's hard to resist writing everyone's name down. But there was one area in which Stirling Moss had the better of Fangio. After winning a race, Fangio and the mysterious lady he always had with him celebrated with dinner and drinks. The unmarried Stirling Moss would go out and have a shagfest. "Popsies," he called the girls. That's the way to do it! They reckon it was rubbing his head up and down on the headboard so much that made him bald.

Then came the Beatles. And with them, Lotus, Jim Clark, and Colin Chapman. Two handsome, brilliant men, and they were British; Clark came from the Scottish town of Duns, and Chapman looked like David Niven. They dominated racing in the sixties, whether it was in a little Lotus Cortina Mk1 or their Formula 1–2 cars. Chapman was a known fanatic on keeping the car light, to the point that when a car had finished a race, if it hadn't fallen to pieces a hundred yards past the checkered flag, he'd get mad. It was great to be a teenager then. Britain ruled the world of racing and music, and we still had an army that could fill Wembley Stadium.

Clark was a farmer, and he drove every week to test and race Lotus cars, and then on Monday after the races he'd drive home again, about 320 miles. His driving style was like his nature: cool, calm, and humble. It was deceiving, too, because he was terrifically fast and smooth. The man was legend. He was twice world champion, and, sadly, died during a Formula 2 race at Hockenheim, Germany, on April 7, 1968. On the fifth lap, he veered off the track at

150 mph. They still don't know what happened. He was only thirty-two years old.

In 2000, I raced my Lotus Cortina Mk1 at Daytona, and it was number 21, Jim Clark's old number, and the same color scheme. I got a podium place, and I met Jim Clark's widow, Sally, in between races. She singled me out, held my hand, and said, "Jim would have been proud of you." She was misty-eyed and I choked up. I enjoyed that tear.

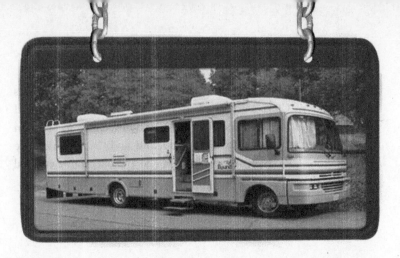

The Bounder Unleashed

TOO HUGE TO DRIVE

About ten years ago, I flew up to Chicago to race at a brand-new track called Gingerman Raceway. I was meeting my buddy Tim Tyrrell, ex–All American footballer, ex–LA Rams, ex–Cleveland Browns. He had picked up a motor home that I'd rented and was going to bring it to the airport. Then I was going to drive the 120-odd miles to the track.

Tim had stocked the fridge with beer and wine and sandwiches. Tim's a big lad, and he thinks everybody eats like him. "Hey, Brian, I got some good vittals for ya! Check this out." He'd bought some shrimp. They were the size of a baby's wrist and just as long. "Holy shit, Timmy! How did you get the fridge door shut?" I should have known that Timmy was a "Special Teams" player (this means you have to be mad, fearless, and very, very strong). "Well, there's your map. See ya, and good luck!"

The motor home was called a Bounder. It was friggin' huge. It was too wide for the chassis and too long for the wheelbase. It had enormous mirrors, about two-feet long. And pretendy wood throughout.

My mission was to drive to Gingerman, which was on the other side of Lake Michigan, and rendezvous with Thomas and my brother Maurice, who had trailered up the Lotus Cortina. They didn't have a hotel, so it was imperative I got there. Oh-oh! It's already four thirty P.M. and I have a long way to go.

I finally get out of the airport and on to the freeway. The Chicago rush hour is just beginning. It's absolutely jammed, and I am just getting used to the width of this thing. It's a bit like punting a whale down the River Cam. Bloody hell, that truck was close! Too close! It's getting dark, I'm trying to find road signs, trucks are attacking me at every opportunity, and the noise of the flippin' cutlery and the blinds rattling and the cupboard doors banging open and shut was getting me just a tad snippy when—BANG! A truck takes off my nearside wing mirror. It's an electric one, and now it's hanging by the wires, banging and bashing against the bodywork. Oh joy! Now I've got the whole fucking orchestra and I can't stop.

After about four hours, the traffic thinned to a 30-mph cruise. I was worried about the boys. They had no food, and Gingerman was out in the boonies. I finally left the interstate and started to ask at garages where the track was. "Never heard of it" was the general response. Well, somebody's gotta know, but nobody did. It was about ten at night when I called the boys. "I still can't find the road." They couldn't help me, because they had driven in in daylight and a farmer had shown them the way. Bollocks, what am I gonna do? There was a Wendy's ahead. I asked there, and a little kid said, "Sure, mister, you go down that road there." "Thanks, kid! Here's ten bucks," I said.

Nearly there. I phone again. "Guys, I'm nearly there." "Hurry up, we're starving! And it's pitch-black. And there's no sign for the track because it's new." "Okay. I'm about five miles away." I drive down the road, and there is a big sign: ROAD CLOSED.

"Oh, hell's bells and buckets of shit—no, not bloody now!" So I did what every man would do. I moved the barriers and continued down the road. Turned out there was a very good reason for the closure. They were repaving the road. There were holes the size of Holland. The Bounder was rolling and bucking like a covered wagon. After three miles, I was getting worried. It was pitch-black out there, then suddenly I saw the light from a torch. It was them. They were jumping up and down and waving—I'd made it. No wonder nobody knew where it was. It was a bit like Croft Aerodrome all those years ago—a bloody field in the middle of nowhere, with no signs. The boys were very happy to see me.

The Bounder looked like it had been attacked by Apaches. Mirror hanging off, cutlery and plates all over the floor, mud from the potholes everywhere. But it was warm. We set up the bus, started the generator, put in the *Blade Runner* DVD, opened the wine, and ate the food. Then it started to rain, and it didn't stop for ten hours.

The next day, there was a quagmire outside. Thomas said we'd have to change the gearing in the Cortina. But where? On grass? How the hell were we gonna do that?

"We crawl underneath and I unbolt the bell housing. You hold the drive shaft and we slide it off together," said Thomas.

"Sounds friggin' dangerous to me," I said.

"It's easy," he said.

I knew he was fucking with me. We got underneath and got started. He said, "Now, now." I pulled the drive shaft back. Christ, it was heavy. I pulled, and the oil came out all over my face, my hair, my eyes. It was black and nasty.

It started to rain again.

After much tugging, pushing, swearing, and alignmentization, we finally got the vicious bastard back on. We were covered in oil and it was getting dark again. The rain was like Zeus pissing on you, so I got a bar of soap and stood out there and showered in the rain. Cleaned up, we got back in the Bounder and dried off. Maurice cooked a shepherd's pie. The rain kept falling, and in the motor home it sounded like a really bad drum solo, and it was gonna be a long one. You know the old saying? It's when the drums stop you should worry, because then the bass solo starts!

The racing that weekend was not a success. It rained constantly. People were skidding off everywhere. Those with very expensive racers just turned around and went home. The only good thing was Tim Tyrrell came to the track with a friend, and he was going to drive the Bounder back to Chicago. The first thing he did was reverse it into a fence, taking off a large portion of the back end (and he didn't even notice). The Lotus had been plagued with problem after problem, mainly the brakes—which will get your attention real quick, causing the old rabbit's nose anal trouble all weekend.

We finally got home, and a few days later, I got the bill for the Bounder from the rental company. The damage had exceeded the rental and they would never rent to me again. I thought that was a bit harsh until I saw the damage report. Tim had even managed to lose the other wing mirror on his way back.

Moscow 1991

PLAYING THE SOUND OF FREEDOM FOR
A MILLION PEOPLE

AC/DC had just finished our last gig of the world tour in the Barcelona Olympic Arena. Crowd's going mad. We were in the dressing room feeling good, manager rushes in—we've just had a call from Russia.

Us: "Who the hell do we know in Russia?"

The manager: "No, from Russia itself."

Us: "You mean the country?"

The manager: "Yeah, the country."

Us: "Piss off."

Actually, he wasn't kidding. Boris Yeltsin had just outcouped a coup and was standing on a tank promising the young people who had stood by him anything they wanted. "AC/DC!" they screamed. So they phoned us and asked us to be there in three days. Now, my charity and imagination stretch only so far, meaning how much? And how are we going to get twelve trucks and six buses from Barcelona to Moscow and set up in three days? It would be easier to shoe a camel.

Anyway, some mention of gold and all the caviar you could eat seemed to do the trick. (Our manager liked caviar. I won't mention his name, because he was a dyed-in-the-wool twat.) Now, how the hell were we going to get there? "No problem!" said the voice on the phone. "We fly down three Antonovs to pick you up." Well, they flew in next morning. Probably the first Russian military aircraft in Spain since the Civil War. The band flew Aeroflot and, yup, it's as bad as they say. Outside toilets, hammer-throwing stewardesses who tell you to "pees off" in Russian, all the cheap vodka they can sell you. And our air crew were cranky because the coup had failed. We took off. The pilot did a barrel roll just to prove the plane really was an ex-Tupolev bomber. He needn't have bothered. I mean, I've never been on an airliner with a Perspex nose and a tail-gun position.

We made ourselves comfortable in our bolted-in deck chairs, and off we went. I threw the air hostess a smile and she threw me a bowl of hot Stroganoff. As we approached Moscow, the stewardesses seemed to look much smarter. They must have shaved before landing. Or was it the effect of the vodka . . .

Anyway, wow! Here we were in friggin' Moscow! Who woulda thunk it, me, Brian "Dunston-on-Tyne" Johnson? We got to passport control expecting the worst. The rest of the lads, worriers all, said to me, "Jonna, you go first."

The lightbulbs in Russia are all 11½ watt, so it all looks a bit, well, Russian—as gloomy as Gene Simmons's next career move. The guard fella took one look at me and screamed, *"TOVARICH!"*

I said, "No, my name's Brian."

Then all these other fellas came and picked me and the rest of the band up on their shoulders and carried us through to the main arrivals hall. We couldn't believe it—there were thousands of people, who were supposed to be the bad guys, cheering and shouting. We were put into our cars—the whole point of this story—which were ZIL limos. The real deal. The ones in the movies (the ones that separate the proles from the Politburo). I wonder who has sat in this bugger before me. The cars were just as ugly as American Cadillacs and just as daft. The ride felt like two wrestlers were shagging each other in the boot. We had our own escort—a magnificent fella on a Harley, I swear, with a buffalo head with horns instead of a helmet and a hide down his back. I'm sure he was a descendant of Genghis Khan. Chrissie Hynde wouldn't have liked it, but I wish I'd had my camera.

The gig went ahead as planned at Tushino military airfield. Our crew was magnificent and TimeLife were there to record it. We were told it would not rain, as they had aircraft spraying the clouds with "Russian secret vepon."

Our dressing tent was just that—with duckboards and two 11½-watt bulbs. The tour manager kept coming in and saying, "There's half a million out there, and they're still coming." Bloody hell, that's a lot of comrades.

Then, half an hour later: "Lads, there's over a million. The authorities are getting nervous, so they've drafted in thirty thousand armed soldiers." I thought, are you fuckin' kidding me? That's dangerous. I really needed to take a leak, so I went outside and peed against a concrete pillar with a rusty ball on top. I was admiring all the old and new aircraft at the airbase in the gathering gloom when two big buggers with proper guns started shouting at me, "*Nyet, nyet,* capitalist riock 'n' riolla, *nyet!*"

They were quite peeved. As I pissed, I nearly shat myself. After our translators had calmed them down with much talk and a carton of Marlboros, I asked what the problem was. "You just pissed on *Sputnik.*"

Pissing aside, it was the biggest concert anyone had ever played. The mood of the crowd was cautious at first, then very feel-good, and then, when the rock 'n' roll started, to these people it was the sound of freedom.

Alligator Alley

HOME IS WHERE THE ALLIGATORS ARE

My first Florida trip was with Paul Thompson. We rented an apartment in Fort Myers Beach. We arrived at Miami airport—the noisiest I've ever been in. Then we rented a car. Paul looked shocked. I'd have thought that years with Bryan Ferry's wardrobe in Roxy Music would have readied him for this, but no. It was a Ford Shitehawk. We had to get out of Miami.

I don't know if you've noticed, but whenever you drive out of a rental car park, you always end up in the area where all the murderers and gangs hang out. I was only shot once; Paul caught a bullet in his teeth (drummers can do that).

We headed west to the other side of Florida, but first we had to get across "Alligator Alley." This road was notorious. It was dead straight and at night you couldn't tell how far away the oncoming headlights were, which made it deadly to overtake. Alligator Alley was also famous for the alligators on the side of the road, so getting a puncture or breaking down was definitely a bad thing. And this car was rotten. I mean, it was brand-new and it couldn't pull your cap off, and we frightened ourselves. Well, I was driving, and it was dark and the wrong side of the road. We arrived at Fort Myers Beach, checked in, and immediately checked out—fell asleep, I mean. We were knackered.

But we'd survived. And it can't have been too hard, as I would return in 1984 to buy an apartment there.

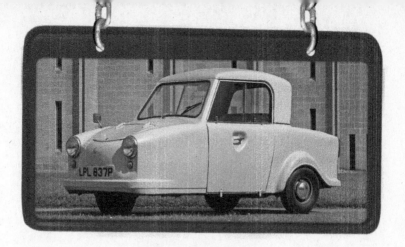

Teacake

HANDICAPPED CARS ARE DANGEROUS

Teacake was the nickname of a laborer who worked at C. A. Parsons, an engineering firm. He had a wooden leg and a personality to go with it. I only tell this tale because it involves one of the strangest vehicles on the road in the sixties, a government car given to people who'd been injured or wounded in the army, or who had a handicap. They were all painted blue, they had three wheels (nice and safe, then), a sliding door, and a top speed of 25 mph. They also had a tiller instead of a steering wheel, so boating lessons were required. Teacake had the distinction of having overturned one whilst tremendously drunk, and he was now banned from driving.

His wooden leg creaked at every step, so you always knew when he was coming, and he was always coming, especially at tea breaks. He was always after free tea. "Hey, lads, got any spare tea?"

Every day he ate a teacake with jam in it. One time, he sat moaning about it: "I'm sick of bloody jam. Every day it's the same bloody thing."

"Well, why don't you get your wife to put something different in them?" I said.

"I'm not married," he replied.

"Well, your mother then?"

"I live on me own."

"Well, who makes ya sandwiches then?"

"Me," said Teacake.

"Twat!" I said.

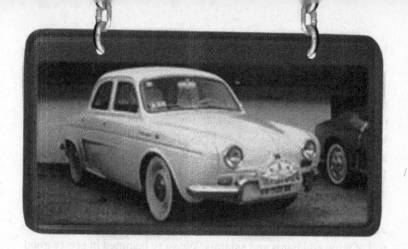

The Italian Job

DEATH AND DESTRUCTION

It was summer 1966, and we were driving down the A1 to Dover to go on our first international holiday, to my Italian side of the family's house in Frascati, near Rome. By "we," I mean George Beveridge, Robert Conlin, and me. England were beating Germany 4–2 in the World Cup at Wembley. What a day! We gave two fingers to every German car we saw. This was the life: three nineteen-year-old lads in a quite new Renault 9—it was Rob Conlin's (he was an only child, lucky git). We were going where our fathers had been twenty years earlier, but we weren't going to get shot at.

We boarded the ferry at Dover, and the cars were just unbelievable: Aston Martin 4s and 5s, Bentley Continentals, Facel Vegas, Ferraris, even a Gullwing Mercedes, all on one ship. We couldn't believe there were so many rich people in the world.

This was a time when you were really proud to be British. Honest. The Beatles and the Stones ruled the world, Minis were selling everywhere, though in Italy they were made under license and called

Innocenti. British bikes still ruled the roost: Norton, Triumph, BSA, Ariel, James.

We were off. The ferry left the port, and for the first time in my life I saw what the White Cliffs of Dover fuss was all about. The drive through France, Switzerland, then Northern Italy, then, on the well-named Autostrada Sud, to Frascati was just wonderful. We had a great time, and suddenly realized that cars were everything to the Italians. The beautiful Alfas, Giuliettas, Lancias. They were a little different.

When we left, after two great weeks, little did we know what was about to happen to us. The family loaded us up with cardboard boxes full of wine and hams and salamis. We were hemmed in pretty good. Off we set, late as usual, and got lost a few times trying to find the road out of Frascati.

After driving through the night, Robert Conlin was pretty tired by about four A.M. He wouldn't let George or myself help him drive, in case "we broke the gears." I swear that's what he said. So we slept as best we could in the car. We were about a third of the way through France, on the dreaded N7 autoroute, notorious in motoring fraternities for death and destruction. We had to get to Calais for the ferry or we'd miss work in Newcastle on Monday. The day was Saturday, and the ferry ticket said four thirty P.M. departure. If we kept going, only stopping for gas, we'd be okay.

Rob didn't look that good, so we volunteered our driving services, but we were denied yet again. George Beveridge said to me, "Hey, how about a swap, Brian? I'm sick of sitting in the back." The back did look like a mobile grocer's, but it was my turn, so we swapped. That was the best swap I ever did in my life.

One hour later, on the N7, there was a family of four having a picnic at the side of the road, by their Peugeot Estate. We had just passed a car full of English nurses, and we'd waved to each other. Rob Conlin fell fast asleep at the wheel doing 70 mph, and before we could do anything, he hit the Peugeot full-on. Everything turned black-and-white; I mysteriously went completely deaf; and it's true, it was all in slow motion: "HOLY SHIT, is this thing ever gonna stop rolling?" It went over seven times, according to witnesses. The roof of the car was flattened to the door-handle level. There was complete silence.

Then the screaming started. Rob Conlin was the screamer: the steering wheel had collapsed and the ignition key had gone through his rib cage. George had been catapulted out of the front seat into a field. I was trapped. This car was rear-engined. There was no way out. I took deep breaths and checked for blood. "None—that's not possible. Ooh, you jammy swine," I thought. The bloody awful French sirens were getting closer. Voices surrounded the car, English voices, girls' voices, nurses' voices. I sat and waited to be rescued, but the problem was they didn't know I was there. They couldn't see me.

I must admit to a smidgen of panic, because the car was on its side, gas was leaking everywhere, and the engine was hot. I started shouting, but I was told later that everybody was looking after Rob or in the field with George, who had horrendous injuries.

I decided to try to get out through the engine bay, daft bugger. I pulled the seat away—not difficult in sixties' Renaults—put my hand through and promptly burnt myself. I screamed, "OOYAH!" Just then a *pompier* saw me and shouted, *"Cet git anglais entre l'auto est FUCKAYED!"* (I think.)

They got me out and laid me down. Shock was setting in now, and the enormity of the swap I did with George. There was my best pal on a stretcher, lookin' so dead, being rushed into an ambulance. Oh, George, don't die . . .

Everybody was looking at me kinda weird, I couldn't understand it. I'd just survived a major prang and they were looking at me like it was my fault. Then the policeman asked if we'd been drinking, and that's when I realized I was drenched in Italy's finest wine. The only reason we weren't done for that was because I pointed out that all the corks were still in the bottle necks. And that's when the pain in my chest kicked in. So I hadn't got away with it; it was an inside job—three broken ribs.

I was put in a village B&B. They were so nice to me. The others were in the hospital, I'll never forget that night. I was alive, but I didn't know if George was. Next day, I went to the hospital. The lads were alive. A little battered, but that didn't matter. We had no money at all, so all we worried about was getting out of there. George had stitches all over his face and was still bleeding. What we did was, I rubbed some of his blood on my face, jumped into bed, and pretended to be George, while George, with Rob's help, dressed in a cupboard. We then proceeded to the train station to catch the train to Paris, with hospital staff chasing us to pay the bill.

A wonderful guy from the British Embassy had got us tickets to England on the boat train, but it was to London only. We had no money for food and, God, we were hungry. When we got to King's Cross, after walking through London with our clothes in cardboard boxes, we got three tickets home by promising to pay the people who'd lent us the money back within a month.

Finally, on Sunday afternoon, we arrived in Newcastle. What must we have looked like—George like young Frankenstein, and me with blood all over my pants? That's when Rob Conlin pulled out his wallet and said he was getting a cab home. The bugger had had money all the time! George and I dragged our sorry asses to Dunston, our home village, about four miles away.

At 7:25 on Monday morning, I clocked on at C. A. Parsons & Co. Ltd., broken ribs and all. George went to the hospital to get more glass out of his face. He still has a piece in his head to this day.

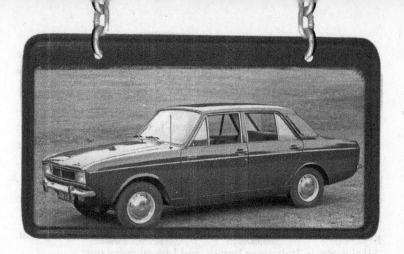

La Dolce Vita

HOW ITALY CHANGES YOU

In 1970, Maurice bought a Hillman Hunter, a white one. (Hang on a minute, all Maurice's cars were white. Even the Lamborghini poster he was caught masturbating to was white. Hmm! Even if he felt good at the time, it must have been horrible to watch.)

"Brian, how about driving to Italy and visiting the Italian side of the family?"

"Ah, that would be great, mate."

"We'll have to take the wives," he said.

"Pardon?"

"The wives. We'll have to take 'em."

"Reason being?" I said.

"Because we're married to them."

I hate small print, but he was right. It was actually a little tough for me, thinking about the terrible accident of a few years before, in the Renault. George Beveridge was still picking bits of glass out of his face. But it was a great two weeks. The sun shone, the ferries were on time, there were only a couple of squabbles.

The family lives on a beautiful estate just above Frascati, in a village called Rocca di Papa. Yup, it's where the pope's country gaff is. The cars on the driveway were just like a magazine poster, with the vineyards in the background. My cousin Giacomo's souped-up Innocenti (Mini), Alfa Giulias, Veloces. A Maserati here . . . We hid the Hillman Hunter behind a copse of trees. We ate outside: wonderful food, wine; then under the stars, then more wine; then under the table.

So this was where Mam came from. These were the rich Johnsons, only their names were De Lucca (whom I name my race team after) and Cristafonelli. These guys had never seen a Standard Vanguard or even a Wall's pork sausage, or laughed at a Robin Reliant. All the cars in Italy were Italian, and I mean every one.

Well, as you can imagine, time went at its own speed—the trip was over too quickly, and we headed home, sad but happier for the time we had had. No dramas this time, just driving back into Newcastle on a rainy Sunday evening. I realized that I never remembered seeing it this gray. Maurice dropped me and my wife off in North Shields outside our damp flat, 13 Chirton West View. Even more depressing.

I had the look of defeat in my eyes, but tomorrow was another dream. Maurice felt the same. "We got to get out of here, bro," he said the next day.

"But how, mate, how?"

Maurice did well. He started his own beautiful restaurant in Tynemouth, called Beaujolais. It was a waste of time, because everybody went to the kebab shop and the Indian 'round the corner, where you could get all-you-can-eat heartburn for tuppence ha'penny. He got into catering for the music and film industries, and runs a huge company called Gigabyte. Bruce Springsteen loves him. And I remember Shania Twain sitting on his knee and saying, "Hey, Brian, your Maurice is a lovely cuddly teddy bear." Of course I wasn't jealous, but later I dropped a red-hot french fry down the crack of his arse. That took the smirk off his face, but not the lump out of the front of his trousers.

But Maurice has never changed. When he first got his Porsche, a few months back, I phoned from America.

"Well, mate, how is it?"

"I'm just looking at it," he said.

"Oh bugger, Maurice, I'm sorry, mate. It's two thirty in the morning, your end."

"I'm just sitting in the garage looking at it, and I can't believe it's mine."

Y'know, not all Porsche drivers are pricks.

Maurice's best friend ever was Dennis, a lovely black man. Maurice and Dennis drove to Italy themselves about four years after our trip. In 1996, Dennis developed a fucked-up version of cancer and he knew he was dying.

"Maurice," he said, "please drive me to Italy one more time."

"When do you want to leave, mate?"

"The sooner the better."

And off they went, two mates for the last time, in Maurice's Ford Fiesta. Of course, my eyes are misty as I write this. Isn't it wonderful that he wanted to be in a car with his mate, to revive the happiest time of his life for one last time?

Dennis took his last drive a couple of months later.

Aston Martin Zagato

WHEN A RENZO MARRIES A ZAGATO

One of the great moments in my life with cars happened in 2004 in Sarasota, Florida, my hometown. Down the street from where I live resides a man called Piero Rivolta. He is the son of Renzo Rivolta. He has long hair, twinkling eyes, and a Billy Connolly beard. He is about sixty-five years old, always smiling as he rides his push bike up and down our little island. We always chat, and he always says, "Ah, Abrian, you musteletta me beeld youacara espezial, *solo per tuo*. I canna makeet for maybe one or twoa million but ees uniquea!!"

He's not kiddin', either. Let me explain.

His father, Renzo, after the war, started a manufacturing company in Italy. He designed kitchen appliances, fridges, washing machines. But the workers didn't have the money to buy cars. Cars were too expensive, so he set to designing something cheap and that wouldn't get road-taxed. He designed the brilliant Isetta bubble car. Simplicity itself, and it even looked cute. The whole front of the car was the door. If you needed a car cover, you just used your wife's DD bra.

His son Piero started designing cars, too. Gorgeous, sexy ones. In the sixties and seventies, he figured that sports cars were way too complicated, so all he did was buy American love-muscle engines and slot them into Italian beauty—the Iso Griffo and Iso Rivolta were two of my favorites.

But the luxury touring car's day faded along with the Facel Vega and the Jensen Interceptor—they all looked like Monte Carlo driving down the road, with Terry-Thomas at the wheel. So Piero came to America and started designing beautiful buildings and beautiful boats. He sails on one of his boats from his back garden to Italy every year, single-handed.

He invited me to his daughter Marella's wedding. She was marrying Andrea Zagato. "Holy Moly! *The* Zagato? The car designer?" "No, isa hees sonna." Piero's son Renzo told me it was going to be the wedding of the year. Oh, Marella and Renzo are designers, too, and so is Andrea, so basically it was a designer wedding (geddit?).

I arrived at the reception. Marella looked beautiful (and very shaggable, I might add). Piero summoned me over. "Let mee intrrroduce you to my friend"—and there was an immaculately dressed man in his eighties, tanned and with silver hair like a halo.

"Emilio, these eesa Abrian, what I wassa telling you." Did he say Emilio? Not the great and legendary Emilio Zagato? I've lusted after his cars for years. Even the quirky ones. I started to act, well, a little bit like a big girl's blouse. I flung myself down on one knee and offered him my fiefdom. I mean, this was the pope of purism, the duke of design! Pininfarina sharpened this guy's pencils! I was having an epiphalectic fit.

He put his hand on my head and said, *"Calma, calma."* I said I already had a drink. "No, no. Rise, my son, rise." Sweet Jesus, he even talks like the pope. I rose and we chatted, and he was just a lovely fella. Later he said his feet were killing him, so me, Piero, and Emilio went into a back room, ordered beers, and had a game of dominos. The old bugger took $7 off me.

The result of the union was the Aston Martin Zagato. You see, on that day, not only did their children marry, but so did their companies. The two kids went on their honeymoon and designed that beautiful car (and did some designer shagging in between).

I was having lunch with Piero recently. "Ah, Abrian, joosta letta you know, Marella and Andrea avva joosta feenish thee new Bentley Zagato." I have a Bentley Continental, and I love it, but I can't wait to see the kids' new baby.

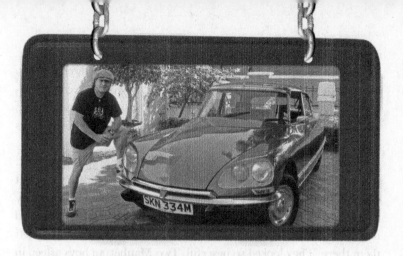

Citroën DS

"RIGHT, I'M UP AND I'M STAYING UP UNTIL I GET A SHAG."

The first time I saw a Citroën DS was in Tynemouth as a child. It stunned the crowds heading to the train station at the end of a day at the beach. The reason is it looks otherworldly. It's superb, it's sexy, it's mechanically advanced and a mechanical nightmare at the same time. The way the thing rises up when you start it is, like, well, getting an auto erection: the car says, "Right, I'm up and I'm staying up until I get a shag."

Well, you know I had to buy one, and I did, in 1998. I still have it, and love it still. It's a 1973 DS23 Pallas, and it's a very French delta-blue. The thing about these cars is that they are used on just about every futuristic movie made in Hollywood, and they look perfect, because that's where they belong. These cars were designed by dreamers, not practicalists, by lovers not shaggers, and there must not have been an accountant in sight. (I think the French Revolution got rid of most of them.)

In 1997, I was in Northumberland in a cottage I'd rented to finish a musical with Brendan Healey. I got a call from my then-accountant, Alvin Hardworker, and the band lawyer, John Clark, who needed to tie up some legal stuff. I picked them up at Newcastle Central Station in the Citroën—they had just flown in from New York. "Jump in, lads, and I'll take you to the cottage and we'll get those papers signed."

Off we went. They sat in the back, marveling at the comfort. "Hey, Brian, first class ain't got nuthin' on this." He was right—it was as smooth as a gravy sandwich. About five minutes later, they had fallen fast asleep, two heads together on the backseat. I tried to wake them when we got to Slaley Hall, but after a while I left them there. They looked so peaceful. Two Manhattan boys asleep in a Citroën in Northumbria—what a picture.

I left that car garaged in the U.K. when I returned home to Florida, but after about three months I missed it so much I had it shipped to the U.S., where it still turns heads. People can't pronounce Citroën properly though. I know I can't. The French say it swiftly, like "Sitron." I pronounce it "Sitrowen." That's why Fords are so popular, I suppose. (The car will soon be coming back to the U.K. to my brother, Maurice, who's gonna adopt it—probably for life.)

In the 1960s, it was President Charles de Gaulle's favorite official car. He was the French president everybody loved to hate— basically because he was a complete twat. He was so French the French couldn't stand him. He was an enormous snob, with a honker to emphasize it. He could speak English but never did, except to say no. During the Second World War, he lived in England and ran the Free French Army—the only reason he was in charge was that he was a faster runner than all the other French generals and got to England first. He even told Montgomery (another twat) and Eisenhower that he wanted to be in charge of the whole shooting match in Western Europe. Much *merde* came from this arsehole's mustachioed mouth. I think that Jackal lad was unlucky, because I heard that not only was de Gaulle a git but he was a very tight-arsed git to boot, which is why the Jackal missed him. De Gaulle spotted a ten-centime coin and bent down to pick it up and the bullet went over his head— making him a spawny git . . .

Where was I? Oh yeah. The Citroën Maserati SM was a beautiful creation that came straight from Hell, if you were unlucky enough to own one. Think about it—Italian and French engineering together. That's like Spaghetti Boulogne, Fettucine Escargot, Pizza Provençal . . . or the Leaning Tower of Eiffel. It just ain't gonna work. There are many tales of breakdowns and engine meltdowns, of electrics not connected to anything electrical. My mate Walt Bohren spent thirteen years trying to sell his, and when he did, the buyer didn't make it to the end of the street. Having said that, it is quite stunning to look at, usually standing still. By the way, anyone out there that thinks I'm looking—bugger off!!

Hurley Haywood

KEEPING YOUR HEAD HORIZONTAL

Hurley Haywood was a legend among racers, five times winner at Sebring, Le Mans winner, and a true gentleman.

I was at Daytona, for the first time driving the Lotus Cortina, and it was qualifying day. I was a little nervous, I'd never driven on a banked circuit before, thirty-eight degrees, and I was told not to try to compensate by trying to keep my head horizontal to the world, but to the track. (It's okay, I didn't understand, either.) Hurley was driving for the Brumos Porsche team owned by the late, great Bob Snodgrass, who was alive and racing at the time. Bob was a big lad, but boy was he quick.

Watching Hurley drive around Daytona was a treat, silky-smooth like he was on rails, never a mistake.

The poor soul was walking past our pit, when he walked over and stood in front of the Cortina, a slight smile on his face. I sat there looking, not knowing whether I should introduce myself, trying to think of what to say. For instance, "Hi, my name's Brian," or "It's a '63 model," or something cool. What came out surprised even me:

"How about codriving with me in the enduro?" Shit, I said it out loud. Christ on a bike, he's gonna think I'm nuts. "Sure—what time you going out for practice? I'd like to get the hang of this thing," he said. Remember, this was the guy who'd hustled 962 Porsches at Le Mans and was quicker than anyone else.

I couldn't believe it. I told Thomas, who didn't smile even more than usual. "What have you done?" he said. "He's going to laugh at the speed difference."

He couldn't have been more wrong if he'd asked a big-breasted Bantu woman for a blow job. Out he went, Hurley Haywood in my Cortina. He did a few laps and over the radio we heard, "Yeehaw, now this is real rock 'n' roll." I asked Hurley what his fee for driving would be. He said it was the most fun he'd had since he was a kid. I paid him in wine (a case of Chablis Premier Cru!). That night, Hurley, me, Bob Snodgrass, Jim Clark's widow Sally, Brian Redman, and all the guys drank Hurley's wage packet. Tax free!

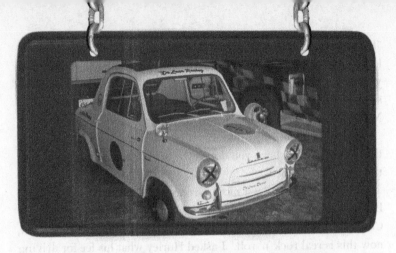

The Memphis Belle

THE NOISE THAT WILL LIVE WITH ME FOREVER

In 2003 or 2004, I was at Sebring. I was sitting eating lunch in between my practice laps, and the track was quiet for an hour. During that silence, I heard a noise that will live with me forever. It was the sound of four Pratt & Whitney engines that lived in an airplane called the *Memphis Belle*, the first B-17 to last twenty-five missions in the Second World War.

And then I saw it. God, it was beautiful! Khaki has never looked so cool. It flew low, very low, circled the racetrack, and landed on the runway next to the track. I dashed over in half-pint, the little car we had for scooting 'round the pits, got out, and just, well, stopped. By now, you've probably realized I do a lot of drooling. Stick a B-17 bomber in front of me and I'll fill a bucket. This thing is, to me, as beautiful as the Avro Lancaster.

There, standing talking to a small group of people, was a tall, thin man. It couldn't be . . . ? It was! It was Robert Morgan, the original pilot from the war. I'd seen him in a documentary made about the last mission. I ran over and asked for his autograph. He gave me a photograph of the original crew and signed it. He was softly spoken, and genuinely embarrassed by his celebrity. I wish there were more like him. I take my hat off to him and all the boys who flew and died in these wonderful aircraft.

Concorde

SITTING ON TOP OF MOUNT VESUVIUS

The band was in New York City, and we had to get back to England to shoot a video, but we only had three or four days to do it, then get back to the States to continue the tour. "Right," said the management, "we're going Concorde." What!! Ah yeah, the thing you just watched in awe, too expensive to build, too loud for the Americans, and, of course, too beautiful and too expensive to fly in. At airports where they landed, 747s and DC-10s would taxi up behind them and sniff under their tails. Honest! I've seen it.

I was an excited puppy that morning, off to JFK. We arrived at the airport and were immediately separated from the ordinary people. The girl who took us to the "Concorde Only" lounge was gorgeous; the girls behind the desk were stunning; the maître d' had a nice arse—well, that's what the guy sitting next to me said.

Aw man, this was it. There was no boarding call, and no babies, not one, anywhere. There weren't any fat people—oh my God, brilliant! Then I heard some cheeky git say, "Oh no, just my luck. There's a Geordie gettin' on." The stunner came over and whispered in my ear, "You can board at your pleasure, Mr. Johnson." Now, I could have taken that the wrong way, if I wasn't a gentleman. Unfortunately, I wasn't a gentleman, and made what I thought a brilliantly lewd comment. She smiled and moved on—I think she must have heard it before.

I boarded. Wow, it's a little smaller than you think. Very cigar-tube, tiny windows, pretty narrow seats, but who cares? You're only on for three and a bit hours. The goody bags were brilliant: Concorde Parker pen, Concorde socks, Concorde diary, Concorde stationery, Concorde condoms—imagination ran riot . . .

Oh, buckle up. Here we go. Jeez, I didn't realize how high up we were. "We're number one for takeoff, ladies and gentlemen." We started. The sound of those Rolls-Royce engines was meganormic. It was a sensation I'll never forget—more power under my bum than I could have dreamt of. It was like sitting on top of Mount Vesuvius just before it blows, and saying, "This is a handy place to take a shit." Then it started shaking more than I fancied, and we were off. Holy shit! This is rocking, this is fighter-pilot stuff. Off the ground, can't see much. The wing's so big!

"Ladies and gentlemen, welcome aboard Concorde. My name is Brigadier General Huffington St. John Hertfordshire. I'll be ably assisted by able-bodied Seaman Higgins, who's my batman, and my co-pilot Harry Thompson, who'll be doing the flying. I'll be providing the fruity voice. We shall be passing over the slow, ordinary aircraft below. We shall be going through the sound barrier at Mach 1, and then on to Mach 2. You will feel a slight push in the back as we go through the sound barrier." The sound barrier—aw, man, I'd forgotten about that. We watched the Machometer. It hit one. It felt more like softly broken wind than the sound barrier, but hell, we'd done it. Then up to two.

The food came; it was beluga caviar, great! Caviar butties are one of my particular favorites, especially with a bit of Daddy's sauce on. I was just getting stuck into my classic French crème brûlée and fourth glass of Chablis when I heard, "Ladies and gentlemen, we are now traveling faster than a bullet from a gun." Immediately I wanted to go to the toilet. A trigger point? I'm not sure.

The toilet on Concorde was exciting as well, but that's a whole other story. Certainly the closest I've come to taking a dump in space. Thank God it wasn't weightless. Back to my seat: food gone. "Sorry, sir, but we're preparing to land." What? I could still see space through the window. We were at 55,000 feet in the air; the sky was black. I was just on the edge of space—now that's got to be some kind of record for a kid from Dunston. Down we came, and landed with a hell of a bang, I must say. Phil said he thinks it was that that knocked his hemorrhoids back up.

Into Heathrow: three hours, one and a half minutes across the Atlantic—unbelievable! Our big old Daimler Princess picked us all up, and off we went to our hotel in Central London. But there was a traffic snarl-up on the M4—it took us three and a half hours to get to our hotel. Bugger!

The Anal Intruder

THE TERRORIZING OF AC/DC

Sit down, children, and I will tell you a tale of terror. Are you sitting comfortably? Right, I'll begin.

Many years ago, AC/DC road-crew tour buses were frightened places. No man could sleep, for fear gripped them all (well, fear and copious amounts of cocaine). During the night, a dark, shadowy figure would slink from bus to bus, looking for sleeping crew members. He was known as "The Anal Intruder." No one could catch him, for he was fleet of foot. No one could recognize him, for he affected a mask with two eyeholes cut in it (but some suspect this was just an old pair of knickers from the groupie he'd just shagged). He wore a cape of scarlet, and had a mouth that salivated constantly (some say it was just old Guinness froth). And on his hands he wore welding gloves. Why? you wonder. You'll find out. He'd leave his tadger out for all to see. Some say it was the size of a blind cobbler's thumb. This thing, this gnarled one, this spam javelin was there for fear factor only.

The Anal Intruder's modus operandi was to board a bus in the dead of night, having waited until the bus lookout fell asleep, which they always did. He would then prowl the bunks until he found a crewman sleeping on his side, then, with a mighty sweep of his left hand, he would lower their underpants, and, with a terrible gleam in his eyes, he would insert his middle finger in the welding glove right up the crack of the man's arse. Then he would cackle and shout, "You know you love it!" Another cackle, and he'd be gone. The crew would scream like girlies, but they could never catch him.

So now you know. It's not all shagging and having fun on tour buses.

We never suspected anyone until one after-tour party with all the crew in a huge steakhouse in Texas. All the boys had ordered surf and turf, steak and lobster, seven- or eight-pounders. Walking to the toilet was one of our boys, with a lobster inserted into the crack at the back of his arse. To entertain the other customers, I smiled over and said, "Hey, mate, are your hemorrhoids playing up?" He laughed and said, "Yeah! You know you love it." A deadly silence fell over the restaurant. It was that voice, the voice of fear, and he was one of our own: Robbie bloody McGraw! The Irishman who is none other than one of the best sound engineers in the world—he's worked for McCartney, Clapton, U2, and many more. Well, Robbie's eyes widened as we rushed him as one.

The next morning we heard from the doctors that they'd managed to get one of the claws out of his arse, but that getting the other one out was gonna sting a bit. But they gave it their best shot. And they told us that Robbie's eyes had permanently crossed during the night.

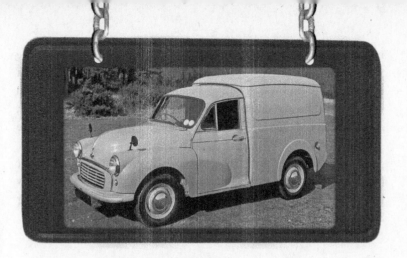

Accident-prone

UNSAFE DRIVING

Dave Yarwood was rhythm guitarist in my first band, The Gobi Desert Canoe Club. To say Davey was unlucky would be unjust. To say he was accident-prone would be bang-on.

One of his adventures happened in North Shields. We were driving around in a Morris Minor van with some gear in it. Dave turned right, down one of the steep hills leading to the Fish Quay. On the way down, we saw a wheel bouncing along the road. The van lurched onto the brake drum and down we went, screaming like big girls until we hit a wall at the bottom.

The tie rod had expunged itself from the spring bob, which initiated metal fatigue, incurring loss of wheel. . . . Well, that's what the mechanic told us. (That's why I love the photos in the end papers so much.)

Another adventure was when Dave was driving a much bigger truck. We needed gas, so he pulled into a garage. Dave said, "Hold on, I'll get closer to the pump." He pulled forward, then reversed. He hit the pump and it fell to bits in front of our eyes. We'd been screaming "STOP!," and he'd just smiled at us. Now we had a problem: Dave wasn't insured to drive. Ken Brown, our banjo player, said, "Get out quick and tell 'em I was driving." That was a cool move, because Ken had the world come down on him: the police, the garage manager, and then his old man when he got home. We were banned from the garage for life.

Davey was—and still is—a lovely guy, very quiet. Things just happen when he is in the vicinity. I am happy to report that he is now living in Toronto—where he works for a company called the Mining Safety Authority. He's their Director of Mine Safety!

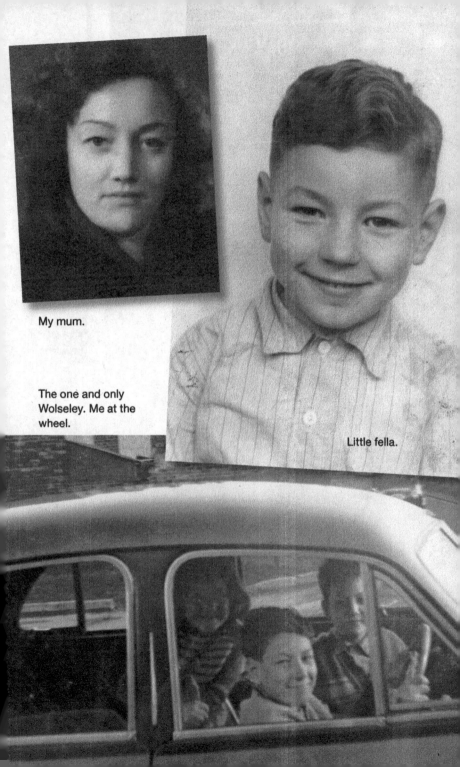

My mum.

The one and only Wolseley. Me at the wheel.

Little fella.

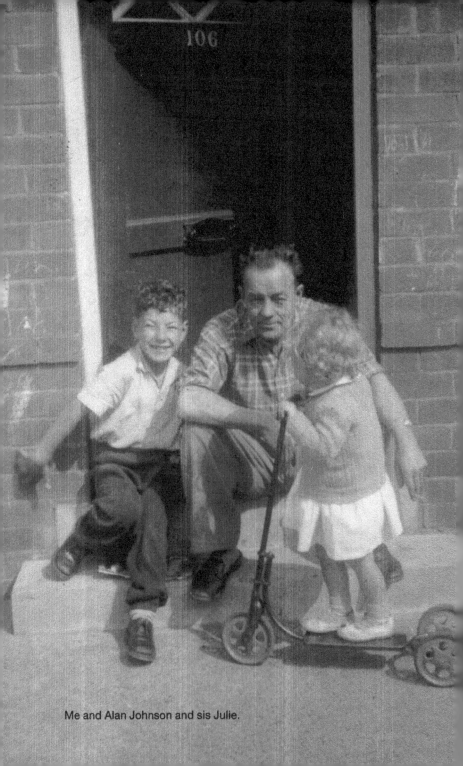

Me and Alan Johnson and sis Julie.

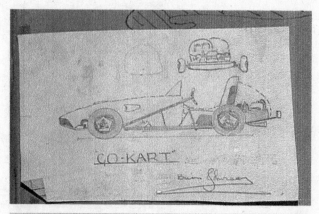

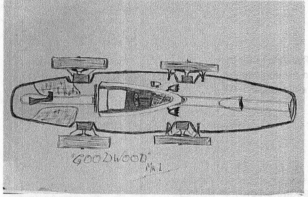

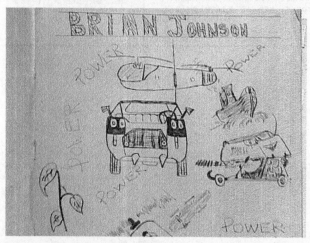

Early dreams of a car designer.

The first passport.

Bearer (*Titulaire*)   Wife (*Femme*)

Name (*Surname in capitals*)
Nom du titulaire

(Mr) Brian
JOHNSON.

Date and place of birth
Date et lieu de naissance

5·10·1947
DUNSTON — ON-TYNE.

Height (*Taille*)

5' 5½"

Colour of eyes (*Couleur des yeux*)

BROWN

Distinguishing marks (*Signes particuliers*)

NONE

Address in United Kingdom (*Domicile*)

1, BEECH DRIVE,
DUNSTON,
GATESHEAD 11, Co. DURHAM

Names of accompanying children under 16 years of age   (*Enfan*

Name (*Nom*)   Date of birth (*Date de naissance*) Sex (*Se*

The Parsons letter that
led to my engineering
apprenticeship.

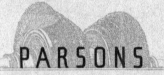

PARSONS

C.A. PARSONS & COMPANY LIMITED
HEATON WORKS   NEWCASTLE UPON TYNE 6

TELEGRAMS: TELEPHONE: TELEX
TURBO NEWCASTLE-ON-TYNE   NEWCASTLE 650411   53-109 TURBO NTYNE

Mr. B. Johnson,
1 Beech Drive,
Dunston,
Gateshead 11,
Co. Durham.

OUR REF   EF/NF.   DATE 11th October 19
YOUR REF

Dear Sir,

      Thank you for your letter of the 8th October 1962 regarding
the possibility of serving an apprenticeship with this Company
when you leave school, and, in reply, please arrange to call fo
interview on Wednesday, 17th October, at 4.p.m., bringing with
you your report for the previous Summer Term, when the matter w
be considered.

               Yours faithfully,
        for C. A. PARSONS & CO. LTD.,

           (E. FORSTER)
        EMPLOYMENT OFFICER.

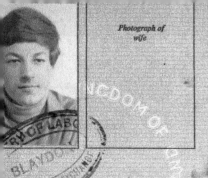

Photograph of
wife

WARNING TO HOLDER

Before making a journey abroad with this passport you should
check that it is:—

(a) Still in force and will not expire before you return.
(b) Valid for the countries you propose to visit or travel
through.

If in doubt contact your nearest Office of the Ministry of Labour.

of bearer
du titulaire

of wife
de sa femme _Mrs B Johnson_

N EXCHANGE FOR TRAVELLING EXPENSES
PREVIOUSLY ISSUED
Amount

ENTRY AND EXIT STAMPS

SURETE NATIONALE
R.G.BOULOGNE s/MER
30 JUIL 6
6.ENTREE.P

NEW ISSUES OR REFUNDS
Amount issued or refunded
(sterling equivalent to nearest £1)

Stamp of bank
or travel agent

My first business card.

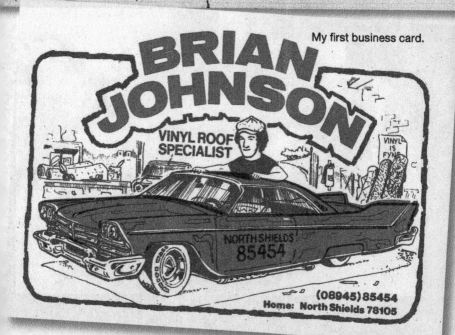

BRIAN JOHNSON
VINYL ROOF SPECIALIST

VINYL IS FYNE

NORTH SHIELDS
85454

(08945) 85454
Home: North Shields 78105

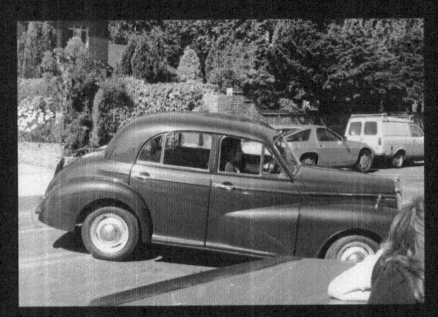

Another Wolseley.

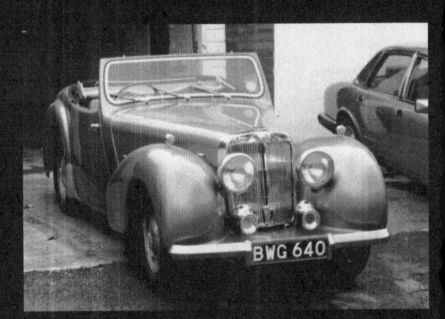

Triumph Roadster.

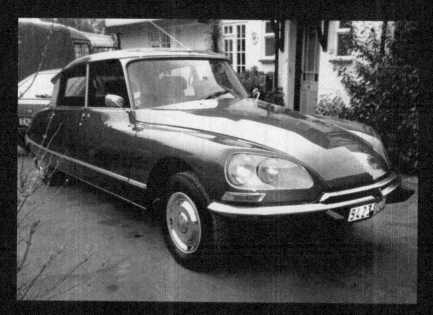

The Citroën DS 23.

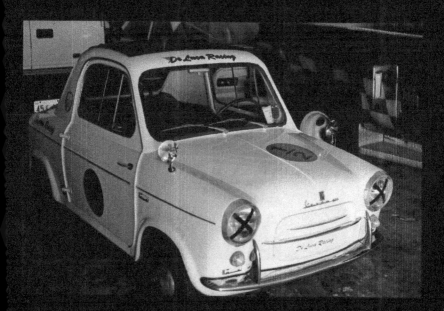

Half-pint (Vespa 300 cc).

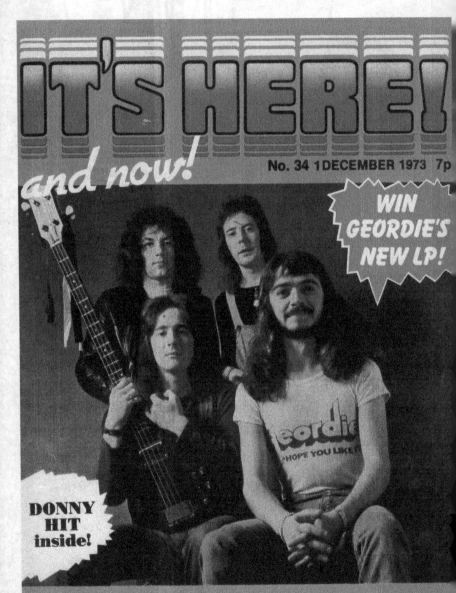

IT'S HERE!
and now!

No. 34 1 DECEMBER 1973 7p

WIN GEORDIE'S NEW LP!

DONNY HIT inside!

THE WOMAN IN DAVID'S LIFE! PLUS GIANT PIN-UP
BOWIE RETURNS! OSMONDS LIVE AND KICKING
PLUS COLIN BLUNSTONE. EDDIE JOBSON.

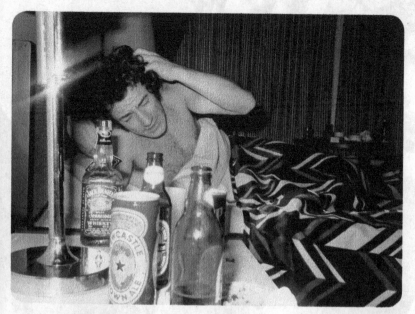

Hungover.

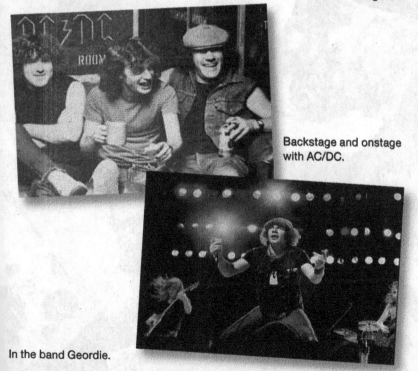

Backstage and onstage
with AC/DC.

In the band Geordie.

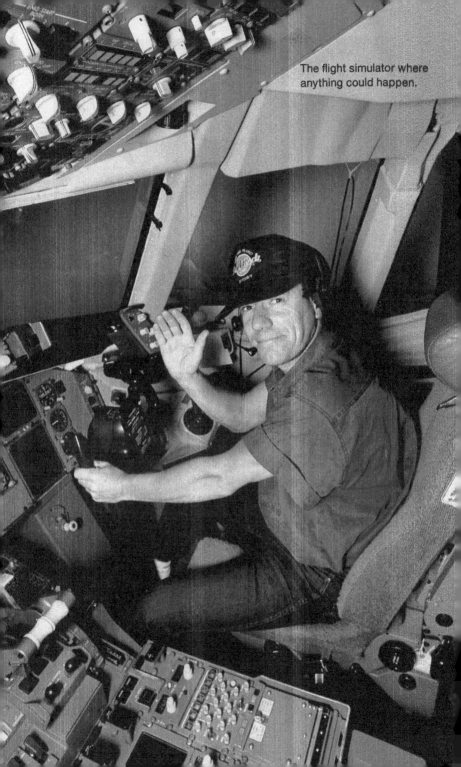

The flight simulator where anything could happen.

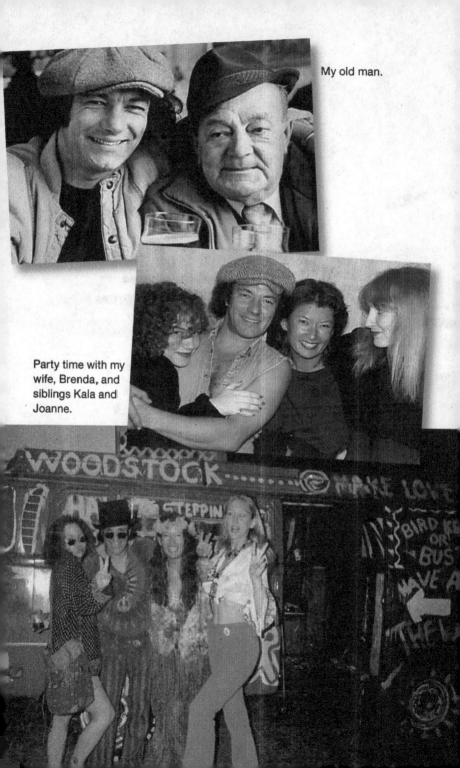

My old man.

Party time with my wife, Brenda, and siblings Kala and Joanne.

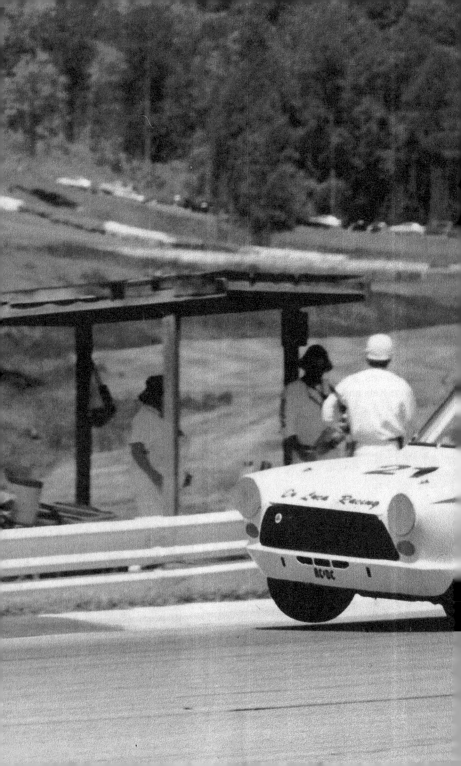

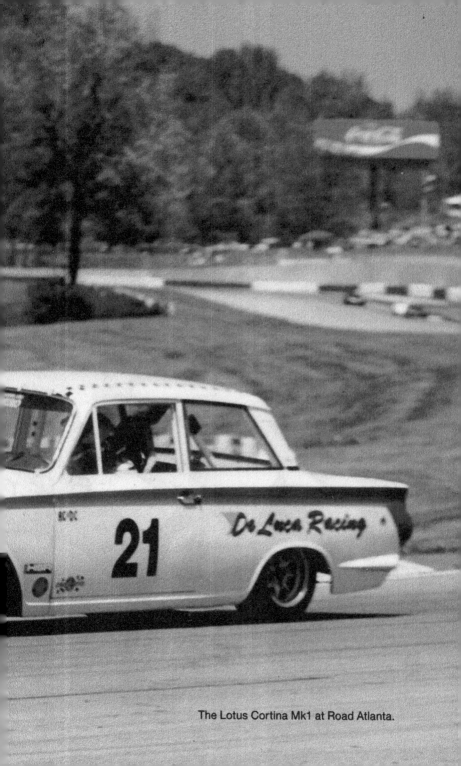

The Lotus Cortina Mk1 at Road Atlanta.

At race school with a Formula Ford.

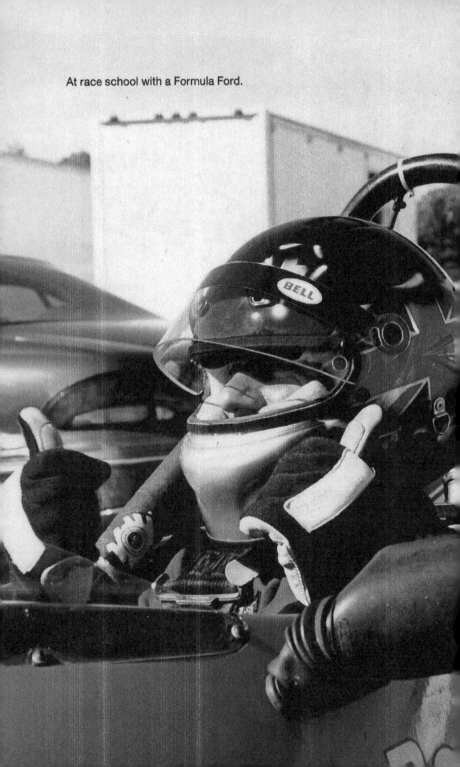

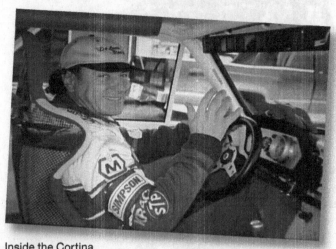

Inside the Cortina,
my first race car.

The Royale RP4 brought me first place overall at Sebring.

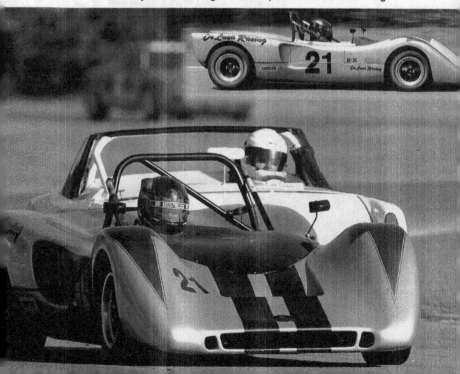

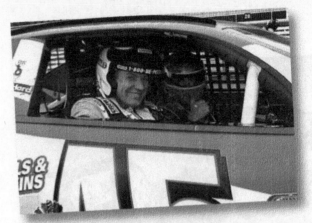

Indianapolis Nascar
training.

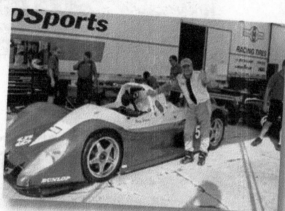

The Pilbeam racer, a lot more tit for your bang.

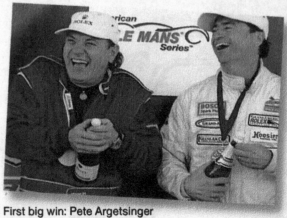

First big win: Pete Argetsinger
at Sebring.

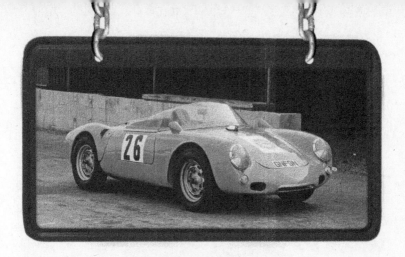

James Dean

WERE DIRECTORS SHAGGING HIM?

Whenever you see a photograph of a late fifties Porsche Spyder, you think of James Dean. He looked a bit of a moody lad. I think he was only in about five films, every one a wrist-slasher, classically rotten. I think the directors must have been shagging him because, God!— the endless silent close-ups saying absolutely nothing. I mean, Paul Thompson is a gabbler compared to this fella. But everyone said he was a genius.

Ah well, he had good taste in cars, if not film scripts.

Cars on Film

THE MOVIES THAT GET IT RIGHT

Movies about cars have had mixed success. Steve McQueen's *Le Mans* sounds like a beautiful idea, but it just didn't work on screen. James Garner in *Grand Prix* is better, if a bit daft, the actors all pursing their lips and narrowing their eyes to get an extra 5 mph to overtake each other. The modern classics are *Bullitt* and *Vanishing Point*, but they don't really work for me.

Then there's *Herbie*, the VW Beetle with a heart. The first one was cute, then the films just got boring as the original idea ran out of ideas. *Bonnie and Clyde* is canny, with all the car chases and Faye Dunaway trying to get Clyde to shag her—what was wrong with him? How about *Where Eagles Dare*, with Richard Burton driving that red Alpine bus and getting chased on the mountain roads? Brilliant stuff! And Laurel and Hardy's Model T that just fell apart as they drove off? John Cleese, in *Fawlty Towers*, beating the crap out of a 1100 Estate, shouting, "You vicious bastard, start!" is still the funniest moment for me. I know how he feels. I've had cars like that, and it does get personal.

The Great Race is another cracking movie that has great characters in it and makes me laugh. Then there's *Monte Carlo or Bust* with Dudley Moore, Peter Cook, and Terry-Thomas, all brilliant, and the great Eric Sykes playing Perkins the Butler—doing Terry-Thomas's dirty work. I even saw Graham Hill in it. The same people brought us *Those Magnificent Men in Their Flying Machines*, with a lot of the same characters. I watch these movies about once a month to get my fix.

Duel was an early movie directed by a young lad called Steven Spielberg and had no script as such, just a story about a car being chased by a dirty big truck with "Evil" written all over it. It was a gas tanker, rusty as a sailor's balls, and you never saw the driver— this is a cool movie. It still keeps me on the edge of my seat.

AC/DC did the soundtrack for a movie called *Maximum Overdrive*, by Stephen King. The film was about all things engined taking over the world. We flew to the Bahamas to record it at Compass Point Studio, where we'd done *Back in Black*. And there to meet us was Stephen King himself, who both wrote and directed the film, and Dino De Laurentiis, the producer. We saw the rushes and came up with the song "Who Made Who," which still rocks. Stephen liked it, but Dino couldn't stand it, which is just as well, because we couldn't stand him. It was about 85 degrees outside, and he arrived at the studio with his coat draped over his shoulders, dark glasses, and the obligatory starlet . . . Mind you, she did have lovely titties. The movie wasn't really a success. In fact, it hardly saw the light of day. But now it has a cult following and no, that's not a typo—I did mean "cult."

Genevieve, I think, is a perfect time-capsule movie, made in the fifties, in England, in color. It was all about the London to Brighton Run in cars from before the First World War (or thereabouts). John Gregson and Kenneth More play the leads, with two English roses for company. Of course, it's all impossibly proper and nobody gets really angry. They say things like "Oh, that rotten blighter" instead of "I hope your next shit's a hedgehog." The cars were gorgeous, and I drooled when I saw it as a kid at the Top Hall Cinema in Dunston. (My mother would not let us go to the Bottom Hall, because the men's toilet was always ankle-deep in pee and you'd walk in there and squelch out. There was definitely a nutty smell in there.) The music for *Genevieve,* by Larry Adler, a harmonica player from way back, is the only thing that grates—apart from the cars' gearboxes. Give it a watch—it's dead easy on the mind and the eye.

School for Scoundrels is not a movie about cars, but it's the cars that steal the movie: Terry-Thomas's Bellini and Ian Carmichael's Swiftmobile. Alastair Sim also stars in this must-see movie about one-upmanship. My favorite part is when Ian Carmichael's character, Henry Palfrey, goes into a car showroom called "The Winsome Welshmen" to buy a car.

Dudley Dorchester (a salesman): "She takes the eye, doesn't she, sir?"

Palfrey: "She certainly does. Can I hear the horn?"

Dudley Dorchester: "Gentleman wants to hear the horn, Dunstan."

Dunstan Dorchester (another salesman): "Of course he can."

Palfrey hits the horn and a noise like a whole troop of Coldstream Guards farting at the same time roars out. However, on the second go, it sounds more like a squad of snails farting. Dunstan rallies immediately: "I've got a temporary flex in there. It's an old type of exhaust horn that runs on helical friction—way too complicated to explain. You either know or you don't." The sweetest bullshit I've ever heard.

It's a wonderful film, very funny, and we still talk about it in the band. "Hard cheese!" was Terry's line in a tennis match with Carmichael. Listen: buy it, watch it, it's priceless. Well, that's not entirely true—it has Dennis Price in it, too.

So, all in all, cars and movies are a bit hitty-missy. Usually, if it's a film about cars, it doesn't go so well, but if it's a movie with great cars in it, sometimes it does. I guess it's like turning sixty—every fart's a fifty-fifty.

My favorite car film of all time is *The Fast Lady,* starring Stanley Baxter, Leslie Phillips, James Robertson Justice, and a gorgeous young Julie Christie. But the main star is a 1930s Sports 34-50 Bentley. Phillips is the used-car salesman trying to get tight-fisted Scotsman Baxter to buy it in order to impress Christie. It is hilarious, as is the line "We used-car salesmen have our honor, you know." When he sees Julie Christie for the first time, Phillips comes out with the immortal words: "Ding, dong!" James Robertson Justice is the girl's pompous father who won't let Stanley take her on a date unless he proves he can drive the Bentley correctly (he used to race them at Brooklands). The scenes of this beautiful car getting mixed up in hill-climbing and chasing bank robbers are so well done that it kinda blows out the window my theory about car movies being so-so. You must buy this movie: it is so well shot you can almost smell the leather and engine oil. And oh yeah, he gets the girl!

Donald "Duck" Dunn

THE BLUES BROTHER

Duck was born in Memphis, and he's a bass-playing legend. Now, this book's about cars but, you see, Duck was in the movie *The Blues Brothers*, and that has one of the daftest car chases ever. Hundreds of crap Chevys and Ford police cars getting smashed up, and nobody cares, unlike in *The Italian Job*, where Jags are thrown off a cliff and everybody cries.

Duck and Jerry Wexler had worked together many times. And I enjoyed their company many times at my house. One time, Duck said to Jerry, "D'you remember the first time we met?"

"Yeah," said Jerry. "It was while you were recording 'Midnight Hour' with Wilson Pickett. I ran in the door and said, 'Stop what yer doin'! There's a new craze going 'round New York called the Jerk. Duck, I want you to jerk every third hit on that bass. And that's how 'Midnight Hour' came to sound like it did.'"

"Hmm," said Duck. "That's right. Jerry, did you ever meet Elvis Presley?"

"Yeah, dumbest white man I ever met," said Jerry. Honest.

Well, Elvis did like Cadillacs . . .

Notes from the Front Line: Wilkes-Barre

It is Sunday, *October 26, 2008. I'm sitting in my hotel suite in Wilkes-Barre, Pennsylvania, and I've just finished a gig—well, a dress rehearsal—with three thousand invited guests flown in from around the world. I feel fit, and I think the band have done a good job after six years off the road. I have just been told* Black Ice, *the album, has gone to number one in every country that has brains, Britain included. I'm sixty-one, and it's the first time ever in my life I've been number one at home and the U.S.A. at the same time. Our expectations for* Black Ice *were optimistic, but we never thought it was going to be number one in thirty-two countries in the space of a week. In the studio, it was probably the shortest amount of time we'd taken to do an album.*

I'm happy because I'm sitting having a glass of wine with Nick Harris, the man who put me through the pain barrier to get me fit enough to perform in front of AC/DC, the meanest, rockingest sons of bitches ever put on this earth. He's also been one of the most important Formula 1 driver fitness gurus of the last ten years, and I met him when I did that pile-of-shit show *The Race. I* had asked him to get me as fit as an F1 driver. After he'd laughed for a full three minutes, he said he'd give it a go. He certainly did give it a go. When I came 'round in the ambulance on the way to the hospital, I said, "How did I do?" And he said, "*Y*'know, not bad, but I think we'll crank it up to ten minutes tomorrow." Welsh git.

But I gotta tell you, it worked, I felt great at the gig tonight. And now, after that message about being number one in the U.K., well, I'm happier than y'know what? I'm not even going to try to be funny. This is too good a feeling to waste.

P.S.: Nick assures me he does not shag sheep! Yeah, right.

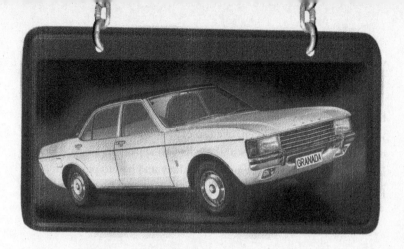

The Godfather of Music Transportation

THE KIND OF CAR ROYALTIES GET YOU

In 1972, we formed the glam-rock band Geordie. We signed to Red Bus Records. We were excited. Fame and fortune awaited us. We would make our mums proud, piss off the teachers who'd said we wouldn't amount to anything, and, oh yeah, there would be loads of birds to shag.

Our transport at the time was a six-wheel Transit Diesel. It was noisy and uncomfortable and very damp. You also risked being squashed by an avalanche of amplifiers every time you braked.

Our first record, "Don't Do That," went into the charts at number twenty-seven. Not bad for a first try. Red Bus said we needed a new van. We couldn't afford one.

"Don't worry, my boys. You're family now. We'll get you one— and a new car as well," they said.

True to their word, they got us a Ford Granada 2-liter V4 and the van of vans, the godfather of music transportation—the Mercedes.

Sweet Jesus.

It was more luxurious than any car I'd ever owned. As soon as we had transport, we began to argue. Who was going to drive it when we were off the road? Then, of course, we found out that Red Bus had done a deal with Mercedes and we had to appear in an ad. We also learned that we were to be put on a salary and had to pay back every penny. I never did make any money with Geordie. I was stone-broke when I left, but at least I'd driven a Mercedes.

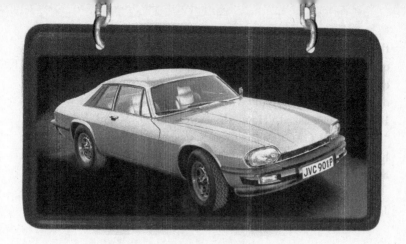

Geordie Defty

STILLETOED SHAGGER

Of all the drummers I've worked with in my life, Geordie Defty is definitely the most memorable. He was as mad as a March hare, especially when you mentioned Jaguars. He was a skinny lad, always smiling. Great drummer. And a world-record shagger.

He had some strange habits though. Wearing his wife's stilettos under his bell-bottoms was one, and when he sat down to play, you could see the buggers. He must have had a nice turn of the ankle, because the workingmen's clubs would be ringing with the wolf whistles.

Geordie was never down.

Me: "How's tricks, Geordie?"

Him: "Smashin'!"

Me: "Eeh, it's awful about that MP found with a rent boy lost up his arse for a week."

Him: "Smashin'!"

Everything was "smashin'!," even moldy cheese sandwiches: "Mmmm, smashin'!" If you asked how good a drummer he was, he'd say, "Fuckin' brill!" There was never the remotest chance of him getting tongue-tied. But it was Jaguars that made Geordie's vocabulary expand like the elastic in Long Dong Silver's underpants. He had an enormously used XJS, with more bumps and grinds than a stripper on ecstasy. His eyes would widen and his Rod Stewart hair would get Roddier when asked, "How's the Jag runnin'?" "Mega!" he'd scream. "Friggin' MEGA! It's mega groovy, mega cool." We would just leave him in the dressing room, talking to himself, a distant "mega" dying away in the background.

Someone told me he now has a wedding-car fleet. And they're all Jags.

The Tyne Tunnel

SHE CROSSES HER LEGS SO YOU CAN'T GET OUT

I want to sympathize with every poor sod who's ever been stuck in a tunnel at rush hour. The Blackwall in London or the Lincoln in New York, it has to be the worst driving experience ever. Like shagging a fat bird who crosses her legs so you can't get out.

The Tyne Tunnel was years out of date the day it opened. With only two lanes, it was designed for misery. All it needed was one breakdown, and the whole bloody thing ground to a halt. I swear it was easier to go 'round the long way. Forward thinking was never a great strength of local planners.

However, the Tyne Tunnel holds special memories for me. In fact, when it was opened by the Queen in 1967, I was part of the honor guard that lined the tunnel every ten paces. A surreal image now, but it happened. It was also at the roundabout, just before the tunnel entrance, that I had the fright of my life. I was driving my old Austin 1100 with my daughter Joanne, who was five years old at the time, fast asleep in the backseat, when the back door flew open and she rolled out. I heard the door shut again and turned 'round. I was minus one daughter. I screeched to a halt, leapt out, and ran back. And there she was, lying in the road, thumb in mouth, and still fast-asleep. Phew, that was close! How lucky were we?

In those days, no seat belts were required, or indeed asked for, and child seats were very expensive and not mandatory. Somehow during the turn, Joanne had bumped against the door handle, unlatched it, and executed a perfect roll. She was absolutely unmarked. Amazing.

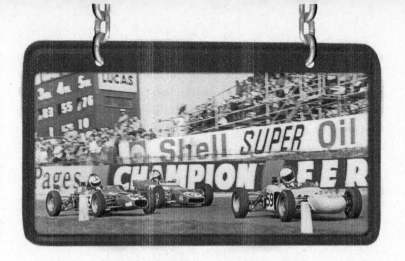

Brands Hatch

SUPERGLUING YOUR ASS TO THE WALL

In 1973 or '74, all the bands that were riding high in the charts at this particular time were invited to Brands Hatch to race. The list included Geordie. The public were going to be there to watch. We all had to go to the race school first and learn how to drive. The cars were Formula Fords, small, open-wheel racers. This was it, this was what I was born for, not that sissy singing stuff. This was my stepping stone to a Formula 1 drive. Boy, was I going to show 'em?

Then I hit a brick wall. It didn't happen. I was slow, I wasn't anything. It was like Kate Moss saying, "Come to bed, big boy!" and you realizing someone had Superglued your arse to the wall. Brian Gibson, our drummer, was much faster, and I was sad, hurt, and un-believing.

Later in life, I realized I'm a slow learner. That's just the way it is, but I'll never forget that disappointment. You got to learn to learn slowly and gracefully, and slowly you become faster, and slowly you become faster than the people who were faster than you at the start, when you were slower. So one day you will overtake the slow bugger who used to be the fast bastard . . . Hang on, I think I'll have another whisky. I think I'll drink it slower than the first two.

Haggis

WHAT HAPPENS WHEN YOU MICROWAVE IT

Somewhere in France, in the year of 1997 or thereabouts, AC/DC were in a crapadelic English touring bus. "All fur coat and no knickers" is how my father would have described it; posh as anything on the outside and absolutely impractically useless on the inside. But I digress. We were tooling along, nobody saying much, doing band things, listening to music, reading stick mags, learning the art of crocheting used condoms, anything to keep our minds occupied, just guys picking their noses, scratching their balls, scratching their arses then smelling their finger to check that it was their arse they actually scratched.

I was hungry. There wasn't much in the fridge—the food had run away a long time ago—but I, genius that I am, remembered that while we were in Edinburgh, I had bought a "boil in the bag" haggis and had got it through customs by telling the guy it was for my medical-theory night-class homework. Now, how to cook this amoeban-looking meaty thing that comes from some part of an animal so terrible that they had to call it "haggis"? There were no pots and pans—how would I cook it? Microwave disasters were legend on tour buses, so I figured I'd boil it in the kettle. Brilliant! I put it in and sat and waited. The element in the kettle melted the bag, and the whole fucking lot blew all over the ceiling, the lads, and everything else. Oh, how the boys laughed at my little accident, but they didn't mind one bit. Mind you, those last three kilometers into Paris tied to the front of the bus got a bit nippy.

The Biggest Winning Margin Ever

FROM PEKING TO PARIS

Growing up, I'd see old magazines, usually in the dentist's and doctor's waiting rooms, that told of great adventures in the early days of motoring. Drivers with names like Lord Percy d'brain Damargee would drive from places like the Horn of Africa to West Bromwich. There were headlines like "Across Australia in an Austin Ruby by Cloive and Sheree Adelaide Smith." Fascinating stuff to fill a schoolboy's head. Featuring a brave and daft bunch of car nuts.

But in 1907, a French newspaper offered a prize for a race from Peking to Paris. That's 9,500 miles. And you've got to remember there weren't any roads worth motoring on once you got out of Germany. They actually got five entrants—not many, I admit, but there were only about fifty cars in the whole world then.

One of the entrants was Count Borghese, an Italian "count" who would drive the huge Itala. Think of the stuff you'd have to pack:

goggles; gloves; a waterproof coat; one box of underpants; a year's supply of oil from Mesopotamia; food; guns so you could shoot more food; beads for the natives; camera and tripod; and film the size of a New York sandwich. I mean, this was 1907. Everything was in its infancy. They had to cross mountains, deserts, bloody Siberia—and you can only imagine what the locals must have thought when they saw these exotic beasts coming through.

Count Borghese had a secret plan, though. He took his chauffeur and a journalist. I hope the chauffeur didn't do all the driving, but the journalist did write it all down and took the photographs. These guys were real pioneers. It took some balls to dodge bandits and dodgy tribes just to race a car. The count came first, and it took him two months. The man who came second didn't arrive for another two and a half weeks. *Forza* Borghese!

Notes from the Front Line: Minneapolis

Oh no! Nick Harris is coming. He's stopping over on his way back from Malaysia, where he's been working with the Formula 1 drivers, and he wants to give me a going-over in the gym. I want my mother!

I have got a cunning plan though. The day after the LA show, we had tea with Ozzie and Sharon, and they were saying that Ozzie's starting a tour soon and he wanted to get fit. They asked who I was using. I told them, so now maybe I can get Nick on Ozzie's case.

Ozzie's gonna love me!

Scientologist Dave

A SPOOKY FUCK

Dave Robson was a fine-looking boy who played bass guitar in Geordie II. I remember Dave because I can't remember what he drove, which makes me suspicious of him. He disappeared for a couple of months and returned a scientolembollokgyst or scientologist. Whatever.

"Dave, what shall we start the show with?" you'd ask, and he'd say, "Really." "Really what, Dave?" I'd respond. "I understand," he'd say. "Dave, what the fuck is wrong with you?" "I am copacetic with your concerns, but things will be things, Brian." "Oh my God, he's turned Injun." He'd just smile at you all the time and go, "Mmmmmm!" Dave had started to sound like an engine that was out of tune with the world, his band, and most mere mortals. He was a spooky fuck.

Things went downhill from there. It was a shame, because the band was one of the best I'd been in. But playing in social clubs wasn't really good for anybody. The audience told you to shurrup in the first set, and then there'd be bingo as the main act, then us again.

Nasty little concert chairmen would shout at us to "get back up and do the songs we want or you're dead." One night in the dressing room (I use the term loosely) of a nasty club called Thornley Close, Deke said to the concert chairman, "Is this wallpaper flocked?" and the chairman replied, "No, kidda, it's good for a few years yet."

So Scientologist Dave and I parted, along with the rest of the band, after I joined AC/DC. That's when the world changed for me, and I knew that Scientology was the biggest load of shite on the planet. The SsangYong of religions—that L. Ron Hubbard must be pissing himself.

Fortunately, this story has a happy ending, and I'm happy to report that Dave has now fully recovered from the experience!

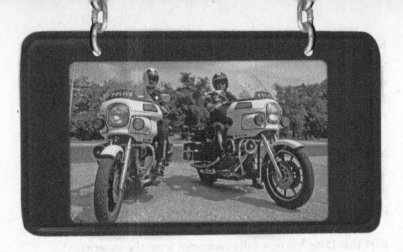

Harley-Davidson

WHAT YOU FIND IN AUSTRALIA

During my first Australian tour with AC/DC, I was struck by the fact that all Aussie car names ended in "a" or "o." Torano, Borano, Ferano, Iguana. Whatever, it was a wonderful place to be, with these happy-go-lucky people, and that's what they are, lucky people. Of course, you can't go anywhere without a ute (short for "utility truck," I think), because the Aussies have a unique way of taking the piss out of everyone. We were in Perth, or maybe Melbourne, I can't remember, and I was being driven to the gig for a sound check in a Toyota Japana when we passed a Harley-Davidson shop. Now, I was told by Moto Guzzi and Ducati aficionados that Harleys were too agricultural to be any good. I don't care. Nothing makes a noise like a Harley. Later in life, in Milwaukee, I saw 65,000 of them go on an anniversary run: one of the few times you could use the word "awesome."

Anyhow, in the window was an HD police patrol bike, complete with red flashing light and a siren pedal. I shouted, "Stop now! Halt! Desist from going forwards! Stop the fuckin' car!" I ran in and asked what the hell a Texas Highway Patrol bike was doing here. The geezer said it was sent over for the police force to try out, and if they liked it, they could order more. Well, unfortunately, Kawasaki sent over twenty and said they could have five for free. Deal done. It was too expensive to ship back to the States, so the police wanted to sell it. They did, to me, and I shipped it to England.

Jackie Armstrong owned a bike shop on Westgate Road in Newcastle. He prepared it for me and off I went. Boy, did it get some looks, but it was then that I discovered that the guys who rode the rice burners and crotch rockets wouldn't even talk to you. They were actually motorbike snobs. I would never have believed it. I liked nothing better than opening up that bad boy Harley when they were parked at a pub. It was great watching them trying desperately not to look.

My second trip out was a strange one. I was stopped whilst riding down the coast road by a policeman in a panda car. I said, "What've I done?" He said, "Nothing, mate, but is there any chance of a ride?" Well, I couldn't really say no, so off he went, leaving me by his car. After fifteen minutes, another policeman pulled up in his car and asked me what I'd done with the driver. I said, "He's testing my bike." He didn't believe me, and it was starting to look nasty when "CHiPs" turned up. He looked a little sheepish, and got a huge bollocking. I got a bollocking, too, just for being me. They left. I got back on my bike and thought, "What the fuck?"

The next day: Hexham and the country 'round Hadrian's Wall. Stunning countryside, wonderful roads, lots of rabbits. One too many. "I'll try to avoid that baby one—oh shit, he's running into me." I'm in the ditch, over the hedge, land flat on my back. I'm winded, can't get my breath. Once again, what the fuck?

Notes from the Front Line: Toronto

Bloody freezing! We're *playing at the Rogers Centre: 46,000. It's snowing and the roads are jammed. Even with a police escort, it takes thirty-five minutes to cover two miles. Good old Davy Yarwood is there, and Nancy. He's a director of a huge company now and he's still got a ponytail. Geddin' there!*

The Canadians have a roar that says "welcome" in any language. If only the border guards were the same. In 1994, Cliff Williams was detained because he hadn't declared a parking-meter fine from London in 1973. That apart, the show goes great. For a huge place, it felt like a small club. Dave's son, Brian, was there. He is now a commercial pilot—what the hell happened? He's just a kid!

Hang on, I'm sixty-one. That's what happened.

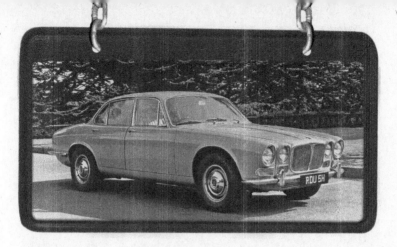

Derek "Deke" Rootham

PEEING IN A PINT GLASS

Deke, as he liked to be called, was—and still is—a brilliant lead guitarist, and played with Geordie II. If he hadn't wanted to stay close to home, he would have been famous. Deke named himself after Elvis Presley's character Deke Rivers in the film *Loving You*. He loved Elvis and he loved flash cars. He had a white 1970 Daimler Sovereign, and he pampered the hell out of it; spotted dice and leopard-skin carpets. Deke never worked a day job; he got his wife to do it for him.

Deke was another of the wonderful characters that I've met through cars and music. His party trick was to pee in a pint glass and bet everybody he would drink it at £1 a bet. He drank it every time and made money. He said it was good for you. Personally, I'd rather cut off my scrotum with a rusty hacksaw. Deke rolled his own cigarettes, the size of a Dover sole's dick. He'd light them and try to get one puff before flambéing his lip. His Daimler, I fear, is gone now—I'll see what he's got when I return to New-"Are you calling my pint a puff?"-castle. Newcastle United itself reminds me of Deke, full of fun but having missed the opportunity to be great, and I feel for both of them.

David Whittaker

TIGHTER THAN A FISH'S ARSE

Davey, Geordie II's drummer, was tighter than a fish's arse, but a nice man. The northeast has its fair share of tight-arses; I think it's the overspill from Scotland. Anyway, Davey bought a two-stroke Saab, li'l red thing. He bought it because it had this thingy which you could press and it would coast along, saving gas. "There's a fucking thing," he'd say. Dave's chat-up lines are legend: "You don't want a drink, do you?" was a classic.

Davey was built like a steroid-guzzler on cheap food; he drove a three-ton truck delivering Calor gas—that's probably the reason he could do a four-and-a-half-hour drum solo. He would break sticks, cymbals, and drum skins all the time, but cymbals were expensive, so he would rivet the cracks together until the cymbal sounded like an elephant with a mouth full of pennies. He was an extremely funny man, and when we were playing rock 'n' roll onstage, all you'd hear behind you (at the top of his voice) was "Mister Grimsdale!" Yup, another Norman Wisdom fanatic.

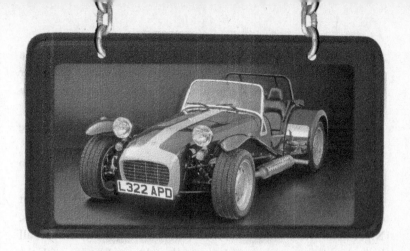

The Unreality of The Race

WHY REALITY TELEVISION SUCKS

I was on my way to my friend Brendan Healey's wedding when the phone rang: "Hi, Brian, ya gotta minute for Alvin?" It was Vicky in New York, the AC/DC management. So there I was, just passing Hexham on my way to Haydon Bridge, when: "Brian, Alvin here. I got an invite for you to be on some kind of Engerlish TV show."

"Not interested," I said.

"Okay, wait. It's a racing show, and you get to race at Silverstone."

"Yes, yes, and thrice yes, my ministerial management maestro."

What a gig. And I'm gonna get paid? I would've done it for nothing!

The wedding was great. It was farming country, so the person at the reception who could throw a Land Rover the farthest received a year's supply of raw tripe. (Second place was two years' supply.)

Fast-forward to November 2006, Silverstone. I met all the other participants.

"Hi, Brian, come in here. This is Nigel Benn, the boxer. He's a pussycat. Just don't say 'devil,' 'drink,' 'gambling,' 'fuck,' 'Satan,' or 'Jesus' in a bad way, or he'll rearrange your nose." (As you can tell by my photos, that takes some doing.)

Then there was "Sir" Les Ferdinand, the ridiculously handsome ex-footballer.

And Gary "Cars" Numan—a fellow gas-head, I may add, who readily admits that his laser-like stare does scare the odd rabbit.

Then Nick Moran, star of *Four Weddings and a Shotgun*. He'd just done the Pan America race—impressive! He looked the business. Nigel Benn was the only one who didn't race regularly; the rest all had a bit of race experience. Les was the odds-on favorite, with the other lads very close. Old-fart Johnson wasn't ranked!

Then there were the girls. Ingrid Tarrant, an absolute sweetheart, who was brokenhearted because she'd just found out her hubby had been shaggin' a lassie down the street, and anywhere else he could get his hands on her. Tamara Ecclestone, a poor waif of a girl with great beauty and a dad with a great fortune. But I do believe she and her sister were his greatest prize. Jenny Frost, a blonde of drop-dead cuteness that could only be matched by her straightness. And a good little driver, Ms. Dynamite, a London girl, I think, who I got much closer to, in the headlines after the race. Also, Melissa Joan Hart, a spunky little American actress, a "teenage witch," I think, who had her own race team. She was definitely the fastest, but bad luck would dog her week. Then there was Denise Van Outrider hosting. She was a lovely lassie, with a "What the fuck did I get myself into?" look on her face at all times. The male presenter was—oh, fuck it, the less said about him the better.

Let's go on to the cars. Maseratis, the Le Mans ones. Oh, they were wicked sexy, hot 'n' horny, Italianly stallionly heavenly! Minis, the sixties type. Caterham 7s, bloody gorgeous li'l racing cars. Then there were the Lotus Exiges—as I have said before, made to race, not to run to the store. Then the open-wheel Formula Ford single-seat race cars, the ones all the greats have to start in, pure penis on wheels.

In between racing the cars, we were to race Monster Trucks—

not me, unfortunately, but I did have fun doing steroid-upped cross-country go-karting on a mud heap—now that was fun. It was like mud-wrestling a car. As in a Robert Mugabe speech, you were covered in shit.

Ingrid Tarrant was to be first away in the Monster Truck, against Gary Numan.

The owners told them, "These things are just about unbreakable and it's nigh-on impossible to overturn one." Right then, they're off. First jump, Ingrid overturns the truck and does a lot of damage. Oops! I see movement in the cab; she's fine. Beyond that, I see movement in the bushes, furtive movement at that. What the—? Uh-oh, guess who? Men with cameras, "papascumerra" with names like "Rat." Then this guy whispers to me, "Hey, Brian, give us the dirt and we'll pay you well. Here's my card." I wasn't too pleased. After I told him to piss off in nine languages, he disappeared into the murk where he belonged. One of England's national tabloid embarrassments.

Once again, European tour buses rear their crap heads. There were two of 'em at Silverstone, and they were in a compound surrounded by a wire fence and eight guards, so we couldn't get out at night. This was crazy. I said, "Where are we going to sleep?"

"Oh, you have a bus each," said an assistant. There were sixteen assistants and no bosses. I smelled poontang. I got the boys on the bus and immediately organized an escape committee. This was a bus with coffin-size bunks. Lift your head an inch, and bang! Get an erection, and you're shaggin' the roof of the bus. Well, at least you can't roll out of bed.

There was a huge camera on a stand in front of the bus that moved by remote control. So we were to be observed, and all arguments recorded for public consumption. It hit me that they were trying to make a reality show out of racing. I coulda boiled a kettle at ten paces!

Then I looked closer at the inside of the bus. Aha! I saw a wire sticking out of the roof. I pulled it out—a microphone! Further investigation revealed more cameras and mics. The bus was a trap; their plan—no drink, cold showers, etc. David and I thought it was a plot to get everybody pissed off, thereby causing arguments they could film. "Does it all end here for Tamara?" they could spout. Then let's get a close-up on her eyes in case there's a teary moment—the vultures! Aneeway . . . David smuggled three bottles of beer into my bag, and I promised him I would never tell anybody about it . . . Oh shit!!

If it wasn't for the chance of driving all those fabulous cars at Silverstone, I would've left, but I gritted my teeth. Next day was the Mini race, which I won. Eddie Irvine and David Coulthard said I was "in the purple." I think that means as smooth as the pope's underpants. I moved up the points board to third.

Next day, the Lotus race, and I come second in the rain to Gary Numan. Ooh, this guy's smooth as a gravy sandwich, but my points go up. Suddenly people are taking notice of the old fart.

Next day, the Caterhams. I was looking forward to this. The race starts. At turn two, Nigel Benn spins, and I can't get outta the way. I spin, too. We're off, and have to catch the pack. I leave Nigel and start picking my way through, and there are my quarries, Les Ferdinand and Gary Numan, duking it out at the front. Oh, this is going to be fun.

I go up to overtake Gary on the inside of turn one; he brakes hard, locks up, and goes straight through the corner. Just Les now. Ooh, Les, it's your Uncle Brian come to gobble up your arse. Then they threw a red flag, meaning stop, so they could pull Gary from the gravel and he could restart the race. Never mind, we're off again; and as usual it's me, Gary, and Les tussling for the lead. I think I'm going to hang and wait for an opportunity; these guys are going to put themselves out. Au fucking contraire! Coming in to the left-hand turn, Les tries to out-brake Gary. He spins sideways right in front of me, head turned towards me—his eyes looked like Marty Feldman's with a pit bull on his dick. I think, "Well, either kill 'Sir' Les Ferdinand or go into the gravel. Surely they'll stop the race to pull me out, too."

So I chose the latter, and lost all my points. They said it was too late in the race to restart. The bastards were making it up as they went along. "Sir" Les, magnanimous as ever, said, "Fanks."

The great day came on a Sunday. I was going to race a race car at

Silverstone live on television, but that's not why I was there. It was the history of it all, the auras of all the wonderful characters who I believe had left their footprints in the very air I was breathing. God, I felt happy. Still got a race to run. Gary Numan and I were the fastest, so naturally they put us at the back and the girls at the front. The stands were full of empty seats where people should have been. There were only about four thousand there, but in my mind it was packed.

We're off. Gary has a belting start, but I stay with him. He's first by turn three, and I'm third by turn one. By the second lap, we were first and second with nobody behind us. Suddenly we come to the front straight and there's Ms. Dynamite, right in the middle of the track—not a good place to be. Gary went right, I went left; she saw Gary overtaking, panicked a little, turning her front wheel straight into my right rear, and off she span, right into the wall—and I never even saw it. We restarted; Gary and I went ahead, and had a great scrap. I managed to get him on the penultimate lap and hang on. I won *The Race*, with most points, and he won the team prize for the boys. It was a close-run thing.

I stood on the podium and received the cup from Bernie Ecclestone. He said, "One for the old boys. Well done!" Boy, that got me a woody. I'd wanted it all my life. Oh yeah, I've been on podiums throughout the U.S., but Silverstone! My daughters looked at me, shaking their heads. "Who is this guy we call Dad?" (They'd never seen me race.) I could see it in their eyes.

So I'd made it, I'd won, but I'd had to deal with some arseholes. The night before, they said a person from each team had to be dropped for the final race, chosen by the team boss—I know D.C. and Eddie were not happy about that. But Ingrid and Nick had the bad luck to be picked—for what reason I have no idea. He was quick. They took us to the studio for a rehearsal—I didn't like the sound of that. We got there; these huge doors opened and there were these huge friggin' round things with yellow and red police-type flashing lights, turning around like something in *Star Wars*, down each side of the audience walkways. What the fuck was this?

A turd in headphones said, "Right, everybody, settle. Listen, tonight the two losers will be called out and then meet in the middle, hold hands, and turn and walk through the smoke into the light, while we play some sort of music."

There was stunned silence. Then there was me: "Losers? Fuckin' losers?" I screamed. "There's no losers here. These people just didn't make the team, you prick. They've been putting their fuckin' bodies on the line on that racetrack, and you call them losers!" With that, I ran to a spaceship thingy, turned it over, and kicked out every light I could. Then, into the face of the owner of the voice in the headphones, the cause of my tirade: "Now you, you useless cunt." There, I've said it. "Have you got a plan B? Because I'm marching everybody out of here until you have!"

I could see the look of shock on my fellow racers' faces, because that's what we were by then: good or bad, we were racers. We walked out as one! And there was only an hour to go before it went out live. And I know the sphincters of the hidden producers in the control room were going like rabbits' noses. They'd just forgotten about dignity. Everybody has their own level, and the TV people wanted to take it away, and I don't think it's theirs to take. That's why I got mad. These reality people tried to demean the majesty of motor racing. You demean that, then you denigrate the honor of all the men who died racing, and that pisses me off. I shoulda stuck with my first answer: "Not interested."

Still, I made some good friends on the show, Eddie Irvine and David Coulthard among them. D.C. got the shitty end of the lollipop: he had to coach the girls. Eddie had the slightly easier job of coaching the boys. Eddie's not a male chauvinist pig—more of a male-chauvinist rutting rhino. He'd fuck the crack of dawn if he could get up in time.

One good thing was that I was the oldest one there and I won. It was a cool feeling winning at Silverstone, live on telly, and getting the cup from Formula 1 supremo Bernie Ecclestone. Nigel Benn and Les Ferdinand are just lovely fellows, except when young Nigel would punch me in the arm jokingly. Owww! As welcome as a blow job from a saber-toothed tiger. Man, it hurt. Les Ferdinand is impossibly handsome and impossibly fit. All the girls were cool and the guys, Gary Numan and Nick Moran—it was a fun time.

I don't mean to blow smoke up anyone's arse, but these two guys, Eddie and David, left an impression on me. They were normal blokes; they were fun. They meant what they said and they said what they meant—not a habit shared by many sportsmen these days. They were handsome, rich, and could probably shag every girl on the planet (and Eddie has certainly tried), but they are gentlemen and they are as "fast as fuck."

Geordie

STARTING A BAND IN A LOUSY YEAR

1976—what a lousy year for me, and for everybody who bought an English car. British Leyland were letting loose the dogs on the British public: Marinas, Allegros, the Wedge, even the tarted-up Triumph Dolomite.

But Red Robbo and Co. weren't the only ones building crap cars (or, as often as not, not building them). New to British roads were the Ladas and the Polski Fiats, sixties cars made in the seventies in Poland and Ladania or something—Communist countries—and the northeast was full of them. Miners especially loved people to see them driving their Comrade cars. I loved the jokes: What's the difference between a Lada and a sheep? It's not half as embarrassing getting out the back of a sheep. Or: A guy went to a scrap yard and asked the man, "Do you have a windscreen for a Lada?" The man replied, "That seems a fair swap." My next-door neighbor George had one, but he was a health inspector and a strong union member, of the "health through strength is the way forward" mentality.

Jaguars were breaking down more times than Dick Van Dyke's

accent. Everything in the U.K. was unreliable. AA men had even resorted to using Renault vans so that they had a chance of getting to you—well, at least before the Renaults rusted away under them. The Queen's Jubilee was coming next year, and it didn't feel like there was much to be jubilant about. Rovers looked and acted naff; there were ridiculous police cars, pale blue Allegros that looked like a parrot's arse. We still only had three TV channels, and the telly stopped about eleven thirty P.M. There was nothing on during the day but *The Mr Men Show*. I should know. I was out of work and had to watch it.

Outside on my drive was a chocolate-brown 1968 VW Beetle, which I painted myself so's the cops wouldn't see all the bloody rust. I had no money, a pretty lousy marriage, two kids I adored (and still do), and nothing else. My mortgage payments were in the bowler-hatted-man-knocking-on-the-door-with-two-blokes-called-John category. There was danger in the air; something had to be done. A revolution, perhaps. Like-minded fellows in dire straits, such as myself, we could change Britain, give it a kick up the arse, make British cars great again, make our voices heard, march to London. Oh, hang on, the Jarrow boys tried that, got them absolutely nowhere. Perhaps I could become a brigand, light the torch of liberty—but I couldn't, because I had no money. So I started a band instead.

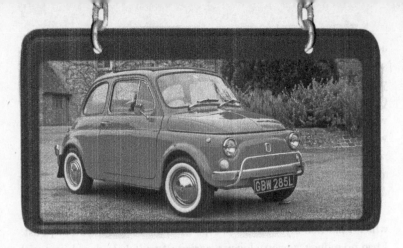

Fiat 500

A CAUTIONARY TALE

I had the Fiat 500 just at the tail end of Geordie. It seemed like a good idea at the time. It was lying in the back of Brian Gibson's dad's garage, a back-alley business right across from Newcastle City Hall. There were lots of those garages around then, run by men in filthy overalls, with some vacant-eyed Neanderthal under a car shouting, "I'm busy!" "Dodgy" was the word to describe these setups. Anyway, this Fiat looked bodily quite good, so I asked Brian's dad to paint it and give it a good going-over, but he thought a good going-over meant painting it. (See what I mean? You're beat before you start.)

It looked cool in orange, the only color he had cheap, but on the way home it broke down, wouldn't start, took a crap, and stopped. There were no mobile phones then, and my carrier pigeon had run away from home, so I went to a phone box and told Mr. Gibson that I hadn't even made it home. He came with a car, tied it to my front bumper with a rope, and drove off. It was wonderful, sitting there, watching the whole front of a Fiat 500 bouncing down the road while I and the rest of that piece of shit were stationary. I never bought another Fiat.

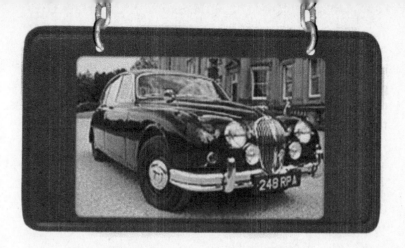

Jaguar 2.8 Mk2

OWNING A CAR YOU CAN'T AFFORD

In the last year of the band Geordie, I bought a beautiful, pale-blue metallic, used Jag Mk2 with overdrive. God, what a beauty! I had to borrow the money from our management to buy it and was paying them back monthly. It was the first luxury car I had ever had. With red leather seats and a wood dashboard, it truly was the twelve-times table of cars.

The problem was that my heart had ruled my wallet and I really couldn't afford to run it. I know we had three top-ten hits, but the truth is we weren't seeing much of the money from them. We were on a paltry weekly salary. I remember one night at the BBC's Shepherds Bush studios, after filming *Top of the Pops* (the U.K. equivalent of *American Bandstand*), it was about eight forty-five P.M. All the lads had gone ahead to their various ports of call in the car. I suddenly realized I had no transport and no money for a cab. I resigned myself to taking the bus back to shithole Hackney. As I was standing at the bus stop, Slade, who'd also been appearing on *TOTP* that day, drove past in their black Daimler.

I put my head down, and the rest of me went down with it. It was just too embarrassing—I knew I had to leave. I knew the band were going nowhere, so here I was, unemployed, with no cash, a mortgage to pay . . . sound familiar? I think every musician in the world's said that, but bollocks, this is getting morbid! What to do next?

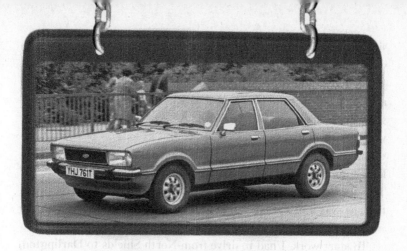

Windshields

A CAREER BORN

Late '76: I knew I had to get some money coming in. I circled the wagons, but the circle was getting smaller and smaller and there was a danger of them disappearing up my own arse. I checked one of the local rags, whose motto was: "Don't let the truth get in the way of a good story," or, "Headline first, truth later." My dealings with them later bore that out. They did, however, have a jobs section, which, along with the crossword, were about the only accurate thing.

I saw an ad for a windshield fitter. I couldn't go back to Parsons; it would have been too embarrassing after being on TV with Geordie. I thought it couldn't be that difficult; I had been an engineering apprentice and a draftsman. On the plus side, I'd get to work with loads of cars. I knew there was something strange about it all when I phoned the number in the ad and a man called Peter said, "Okay, we're holding interviews in the car park at Chester-le-Street service station on the A1M." At the interview, I gave him the details of my previous work, missing out the Geordie years, and he looked puzzled, said I seemed a little overqualified, and signed me on. Funny thing was, he never asked me if I could fit a windscreen to a car.

So Peter saddled me with the cream of British workers, the "I'm all right, Jack" of the blue-collar nation. He put me in for the first week with a man called Norman, a henpecked, hate-filled bloke whose only aim was to make each job last as long as possible. Conversation was like talking to a trained turnip. He wore glasses with lenses imported from Zeiss in Germany, and he had teeth like the Thames floodgates, a smile that would see off Dracula. Other than that, he was a nice man. I asked him if he was married. He said he was and that his wife looked like a bulldog sucking a wasp. Hmm.

To start work, I had to drive from North Shields to Darlington, where the headquarters of Windshields Ltd., Northeastern Branch, was located. I needed the money. Two years earlier, I'd been playing at the London Palladium or the Melbourne Cricket Ground in Australia to thousands. But things hadn't worked out. Still, at least nobody recognized me, because I'd taken to wearing a cap!!! Pulled tight over my eyes, so the truth is now out. Darlington is a shithole designed by shitheads when they were in a really shitty mood. The people talk with a mixture of Yorkshire, Sunderland, Durham, and Seal accent, and that's not half the story. The reason they're not happy is because they're right next door to a place called Hartlepool, and no, I'm not going to mention the monkey.

After a week of intensive training with Norman—"Take ya time, lad, ya don't wanna make it look easy." "But Norman, it is easy!"—I could do the work blindfolded with a pint in my hand. Then, after a couple more weeks, I was summoned to Peter's office, up the wooden stairs of a cardboard office in a warehouse. "Well," he said, "I like the cut of ya gib, m'boy, you've got what it takes to be a windshield fitter. I might even let you do sunroofs, but let's not get ahead of ourselves. Broken windscreens are our means of survival. Remember, every car you see at the side of the road without getting called out is five pound in your pocket. I would like to present you, Brian Johnson, the keys to that Ford Transit, complete with orange flashing light. It came from our Oldham branch and it's only got 85,000 miles on the clock."

To me, it was everything: free ride, free gas, and even a CB radio with my own call sign, Whisky Oscar One One One—difficult to pronounce with a hangover. One of the other fitters advised me to buy a bag of gravel to lay down at roundabouts so people would get their screens broke from the guys in front. (In Britain, cars were fitted with toughened windscreens, which shattered when hit, usually into the faces of the passengers. Most European cars had the laminated ones that just cracked and were safer.) I wouldn't do that though, because it was to break cars on purpose, a crap way of making money. The fitter was a good guy, though, a Liverpudlian who'd made his way to Darlington and then lost his map. (He was definitely dyslexic, a card-carrying member of the DNA, the National Association of Dyslexics. He was also an atheist insomniac and would lie awake all night wondering if there was a dog.)

The adventures at Windshields were great: lonely nights at Scotch Corner, rain and wind whipping around you as you tried to put in, on your own, a windscreen for a Volvo or Scania truck. The windscreens were about ten feet wide and nearly three feet high, and it was cold as hell standing on top of your Transit getting the bugger in. But I really did enjoy helping people out. I felt I was a medic for motors and trucks. Kidding aside, I really had more fun in that year and a bit than I can remember.

One time I was called out to a car that had both front and rear screens broken. I rushed there and found the driver sitting in the boot, legs dangling over the edge, drunk as a newt. He was drinking miniature bottles of whisky, for he was a whisky salesman. "Are you okay, mate?" I asked. "Okay? Okay? Oh, fucking bastard boy, no. I've just shit my pants and its starting to dry." "That's gonna itch," I replied. "What happened?" "F-f-f-f-fuckin' big pheasant through the front screen, right past my head and out the fucking back. Never seen anything like it!" Neither had I. I told him, "Listen, mate, here's my newspaper. Why don't you wipe your backside whilst I'm fixing this Cortina Mk4. He still wasn't back when I'd finished, so I went to look for him. As he pulled up his pants, I asked, "What took you so long?" He said, "Listen, mate, when the bird came through I was scared. I mean, I really shat myself. I had to start wiping from the back of the neck." On top of the £40 he owed me, he gave me what samples he had left and some Lithuanian whisky that tasted of plums.

Every day was different. I worked on some boring and some fabulous cars. Ferraris—the nearest I'd ever get to one, Aston Martins, Jags, BMWs, and Porsches. I even had to do a Rolls-Royce. What a bastard that was! There was at least a hundred screws to take out of the dash to get to the windscreen. Still, I did it and probably lost the company a fortune, as it took a day and a half.

I knew the job couldn't last long: you had to be on call through the night once every three days and it was getting in the way of my music. So I had to leave, which was a shame, but I thought I'd start my own company, and North-East Vinyls was born.

The Dog's Dangly Bits

HOW TO PASS TIME ON THE ROAD

Touring in a band can get a little boring, with only two hours of intense excitement every other night. To help relieve this, I have my favorite mags with me at all times, *Classic Sports Car, Motor Sport*, and *Thoroughbred and Classic Cars*. I've bought every one of them, every month, since 1980, and have built up a collection at home, housed in its own huge sideboard in my office. I love the ads in 'em, I love the wording. Stanley Mann's Bentley ads are just lovely. For example:

1931 BLOWER BENTLEY LE MANS.
SUPERB ORIGINAL.
FULLY REBUILT TO THE DOG'S DANGLY BITS SPECIFICATIONS.

I love that stuff. I feel I know most of the guys in there, I've seen their names so many times. The ads themselves are more like motorcar menus, lists of luscious Lagondas, fistfuls of Ferraris, masses of Mercedes, boatloads of Bentleys, racks of Rollers. It takes your breath away how many beautiful old and new cars are out there. The prices tend to loosen your fillings a little, too! I've just seen a Bugatti for sale at 2,750,000 euro. Holy shit! You couldn't even have sex in it, never mind park it. Who are the people who own these cars, where do they live? I guess I should say good luck to 'em, but I can't, because most of them hide these beauties away and only pull them out for some Concourse of Elegance now and again. Then there are the real dudes who race their cars at the Donnington Festival of Speed and other similar events. Those guys are my heroes, because when they race, they are still bangin' doors and takin' numbers. The guys who drive across continents in rallies—I salute you, I salute you all!

The truth is, all these magazines are written and researched so well you can actually read them from cover to cover. I usually have a napkin tucked into the top of my T-shirt to stop me salivating onto the pages. To car nuts, these are horn mags, stick mags, something to get a boner over. Whenever I'm stuck at an airport, on a long bus ride, or sitting next to a shower-curtain salesman from Ohio on a plane, I whip out my trusty mag and put a serious, concerned look on my face.

"Oh, hey, is that an Austin Martin?"

"No! It's pronounced Aston. ASTON!"

"Yeah, that's what I said. Austin Martin."

"Die, you bastard. Just fuck off and die!"

If the car magazine doesn't shut them up, I pull out my secret weapon: *Viz*. This usually has most Americans shaking their heads: Sid the Sexist, Eight Ace, Biffa Bacon, Raffles, the Gentleman Thug, Slappa Tasha, Fat Slags, Cockney Wanker.

Them: "I don't get it."

Me: "And you never will, bonny lad. You never will."

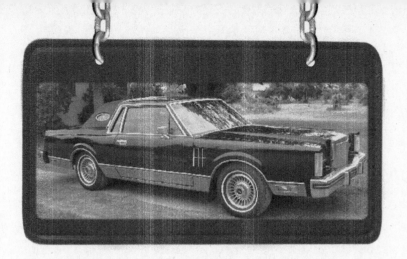

Lincoln Continental

SAFE OPERATING SPEED: 0

The first car I bought in America was what every boy whose first car was a Ford Popular would buy: a Lincoln Continental. I think Jeremy Clarkson said it had a safe operating speed of 4 mph. He was way off. Standing still is the correct answer. But, oh my, the size of the thing! It was huge. It had more seats than the local cinema in Dunston. The plastic chrome was a wonder to behold—there was nothing really metal in this car, or wood; I think even the glass was plastic. I had it for a year; it was six years old when I bought it. I knew I had to get rid of it when little niggly things started, like the roof lining coming completely off whilst I was driving, making me look like I was wearing a burka without eyeholes. I was doing about seventy at the time. Memories of that whisky salesman came flooding back, and I didn't have a newspaper.

The Benefits of Driving in France

Two brothers, aged about thirty, were Siamese twins. They were joined at the hip, but they were happy enough. They went to their local pub for a pint and the landlord said, "Hey lads, the usual?"

"Yes, please," they said as one.

"Well, boys, it's July. You getting ready for your holidays?"

"Oh yeah! Can't wait!" was the response.

"Where you going this year?"

"Oh, we're off on a driving holiday in France. You know, we just rent a car and drive."

The barman looked at them and smiled. "Lads, every year I ask the same question. Every year you go to France. Why?"

The twin on the right said, "It's the only chance he gets to drive!"

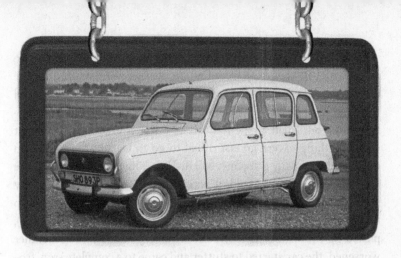

Sexy French Cars

I'M-FRENCH-AND-FUCK-YOU ATTITUDE

In England, French cars have been with us longer than you might think: Bugatti, Citroën, and Renault since before the war. The Citroën Light 15 was the Maigret of motor cars, used by the Gestapo, the Resistance, and the prewar English banker. They were brilliantly forward-thinking cars. I still think they're sexy, that push-me-pull-you gear stick and the I'm-French-and-fuck-you attitude. Anyway, you look at this car and it's beautiful, and I'm amazed you can still buy them as cheaply as you can. They were still building them in England until the mid-fifties. Renault is another manufacturer that built an "I am French, eat *merde*" type of car, whatever it was. The French cars were, well, so fuckin' French, and that's cool: Gauloise ciggies; berets; women that were chic, gorgeous, shaggable, leggy, marriable, slender, and got better as they got older, just like fabulous wines and cheeses; and their bread and their brandy. Aha, that's why French cars are what they are: SEX. Well, you have to start with the basics, and I do believe sexy was where they started.

I nearly died in a French car (remember 1966?); I nearly froze in one, too. In the great freeze of '78, lorries were stopped on the motor-ways the length and breadth of Britain. "M6 Madness!" said the headlines. Drivers were lighting fires under their trucks to unfreeze the oil. I had a blue Renault 4; it was a great cheap car that did everything except go fast. I had to go to Darlington to pick up a windshield for my company, North-East Vinyls. I didn't think the weather was so bad, though it was snowing and cold. So, with my slippers on and just a sweater, I set off on the thirty-eight-mile trip to Darlington. I made it no bother (the 4 was basically an estate car), picked up the windscreen, and set off for Tynemouth. The weather worsened, the car started to stutter and came to a complete stop, frozen up, in between "ah shit" and "fuck me."

I sat wondering what to do next. The trucks going past were throwing slush and snow against the car, and it was becoming invisible. I was getting to the uncontrollable shivering stage. I took the polythene off the screen, wrapped it 'round my feet, and got out of the car. I saw a farmhouse about a half a mile off the motorway, and I was just gonna start running there when a car stopped and a big mustachioed man stuck his head out of the window of a top-of-the-line Citroën GS. I recognized him, this guy was famous! It was Roger Uttley, England rugby player and Jesus look-alike. "Do you need help?" "Yes," I said in Dutch—my mouth had frozen. He got out, tied a rope around my axle, and towed me to Birtley service station. I've never met him again, and he probably doesn't even remember the occasion, but I'm here to tell you: Roger, mate, you were my Good Samaritan.

The Renault 16 was another regal car; it just looked well-dressed always. I still have my beloved Citroën DS23 Pallas, 1973 model. It's a shame such a beautiful machine became known as the "de Gaulle." I know he got driven around in one, but why anyone would compare a Pallas with a fat, arrogant, self-important twit, I have no idea. Oh yeah, and, according to his wife, the general was a completely useless shag.

Vive la France!

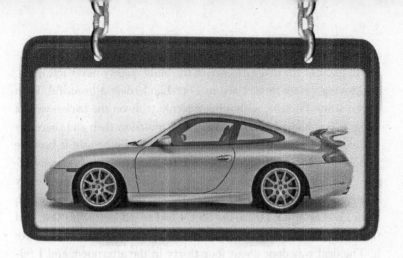

Porsche Twin Turbo

SMOKING IS DANGEROUS FOR YOUR CAR

Now I know I take the piss out of Porsches a lot, but it's only because racing against them is so difficult, because they never break, sort of. Never ever. Bloody things just keep going, as Vic Elford said to me, and he should know. ("To win races, you need the best equipment." He was, of course, alluding to Porsches.) Vic Elford has written a great book on how to drive a Porsche. Buy it.

My very first Porsche was a stunning 944, bought in 1983, front-engined, white, burgundy interior. It had everything, including a hatchback for storage, but something was wrong, folks. Porsche 911 drivers still looked down on me with derision. You see, in their eyes, it wasn't a proper Porsche: (a) it was way too comfortable; (b) the engine was at the front; and (c) it handled beautifully, an absolute no-no for those stupid twats. Oops. Sorry. Anyway, it was so good, I bought another one a few years later.

In 1984, I bought my first 911 Turbo. It was two years old. I didn't want to buy a new one until I'd tested one. Which was just as well. I sold it two months later. If I drove to London, I'd get dead arse, a bit like a footballer's dead leg, and my arse had stopped speaking to me. But the magnificence of the build quality never left me.

Moving on to 1998, I see in Fort Lauderdale a beautiful Twin Turbo white Porsche, with a huge picnic table on the back—well, a wing. It was huge. I had to have it, so I traded in then and there my two-year-old Mercedes Pimpmobile (500 SL). I'd bought it because it looked cool and it had a trick roof, the first real hardtop convertible. The only trouble was I started to notice that they were nearly all driven by beautiful blond tarts who had been given them by rich boyfriends or aging husbands. Shit. I had to get outta this fast, and there was the Porsche before me. Menacingly sexy, I just had to have it. The deal was done about four thirty in the afternoon, and I relished the thought of driving it across the Florida Peninsula, home to Sarasota.

Off I went on a small state road—dead straight and two lanes: B road, as we would call it—running right through the sugarcane fields that stretch as far as the eye can see. The sun was setting, and I was saying "Wow!" when there was the blue light. Bollocks! Pull over. Shite, not a policeman but the dreaded highway patrol. This guy was big, black, with dead eyes and big daft hat that tilted forward like he'd just braked too hard. Unlike in the U.K., American cops stay behind the car, so they can see if you're gonna shoot them or something. *Wow!* became a *wooah!*

Cop: "License, registration, insurance."

Me: "Here you go, officer. Beautiful evening, isn't it, oh ally in the Second World War." Nothing.

Cop: "You were doing eighty in a fifty limit."

Me: "Well, officer, I've only had the car thirty minutes. I just bought it and I'm driving it home, and I was trying to get used to the . . ." Bullshit, bullshit, bullshit. I dribbled on. The Johnson charm offensive was going badly.

Cop: "I don't care."

Me: "Pardon?"

Cop: "I can't afford one, and I don't like anyone who can."

Me: "I'm pretty much fucked then."

Cop: "Yup!"

Bastard gave me a ticket, but I got one back on him, because I gave him my English license, and he didn't know what to do with it, or where to add the points, or where England is. Anyhow, I carried on driving into the sunset. Lord, I could kill a cigarette. So I pulled one out, lit it, opened my window a crack to flick out the ash. Then I thought, "You silly sod, smoking in a brand-new car!" So I flicked that bad boy out the window, proud of myself, till the smoke started rising in the back (shades of Williams). I stopped, jumped out, and there in the lap of the seat was a fire started by a cigarette thrown out of a window by some silly twat. I dropped my shorts and did what any man would do: I peed on it till it went out. Then I folded the seat down and drove home, sheepish.

She Who Is To Be Feared came to look at the new car. "Why's the backseat down?" she asked. "It's an aerodynamic thing," I said. She said it sounded like a "you lying git thing." She lifted the seat and I was copped for the second time that day. I definitely remember getting drunk that night.

P.S.: Porsche asked me how it happened. I said, "Would you believe it, the cigarette lighter flew out of the dash, passed my ear, and set fire to the seat." The guy on the phone just laughed and said, "That's the best one yet." He sent me a free replacement seat in forty-eight hours. Now that's service.

Historic Racing Machines

WHEN IT'S MAGIC TIME

One of the real pleasures in my life is to be sitting in a race car at eight thirty in the morning, sun rising, on a false grid full of historic racing machines, all revving, hungry to get on the track. As they'd say in Hollywood, it's "magic time."

There are so many wonderful characters to get to know. (Also some miserable twats, usually Porsche drivers. Just kidding?) There's Ward Witkowski, in his Alfa-engined bobsy; over there, Super Dave Bondon in his beautifully prepared Morgan; another Brit, Dave Hinton, in his glorious scarlet-red Jag 120; there's Ken smiling away in his snot-green 356. Les, the pit marshal, smiles and gives the five-minute warning. If there is a heaven, then this is where I want to spend eternity.

Notes from the Front Line: Atlanta

Did show last night, another sellout. Throat holding out. Tomorrow Charlotte and I'll see my race team—they're coming to the show. Three more to do, then home. I am bone-weary. I think I lost my sphincter in LA. I'll have to see about getting it replaced soon, along with new eardrums and a foreskin (caught in my zip in San Antonio). Apart from that, the lads and me are feeling chipper. Just heard Wembley and Hampden Park sold out, too. That's cool.

Day off today. I think a sherbet is in order, probably a Jameson's.

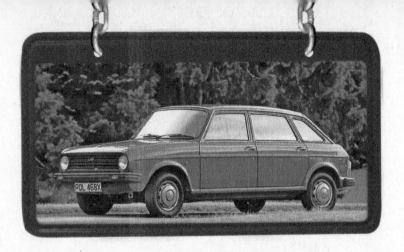

Nnorth-East Vinyls and AC/DC

THE TWO CAREER CHOICES AND WHAT I CHOSE

My own company, my own firm, my own car. This was it! I was going solo. I rented a place right on the River Tyne, next to a car auction room; it was right on the quayside. It was filthy, it was damp, it was overpriced, and it was pre-Victoria British building at its finest. Windows you couldn't see out of, overhead lights that took longer to turn on than a witch's tit, and an echo like King's Cross. I had no startup money to speak of, and no employees to call me boss. But nothing would stop me building my windscreen and vinyl-roof empire. Well, except one thing: customers.

So I had to go get 'em, and transport was key. What should I get that could act as a van and a car and be value for money? I found all of the above in one strange vehicle: the Austin Maxi. Not only did it have a crap name, it looked like a matchbox with a hard-on. It was British Leyland mustard, the color of a chemical meltdown or the contents of a baby's nappy. The interior trim—once again, using the word loosely—was a slightly darker color called "Gorilla Minge." The dashboard was a bookshelf with a square dial on one side, a speedometer, and that was it. The steering wheel and seats were the only thing that told you this was not a skip. But the good thing was the rear seats folded down and I could get all my stuff in there. And it was pretty reliable.

Now I needed someone to work in the office and help answer the phone calls that were soon to come flooding in. I met a great lad called Ken Walker, a big, smiling man who could drink for England. And he had a posh voice and played rugby and stuff. We arranged to meet at the pub.

"Hey, Ken, I'm Brian. How are you?"

"Fer-fer-fer-fer-fer-fine."

Uh-oh! "So, Ken, you've done vinyl roofs before, then?"

"Aw-aw-aw-aw-aw-almost." He smiled. I smiled, too. Who was gonna answer the phone?

"Can you put in windshields?"

"N-n-n-n-n-not as such."

Ken was a bit like the way he spoke; he never quite finished anything except his pint (he was meticulous in that department). I liked him though. He was jovial and fun. We went to the office and I showed him 'round.

He said, "Th-th-th-th-th-there's not much fuckin' here, is there?"

"No, my son," I said. "But there soon will be."

The next few months really were good. People and garages remembered me from Windshields, and I got a lot of their work: the Datsun garage, the Lada garage, and a few other prize ones. Ken's stammer got worse when he got excited, and his head would jerk like he was hanging on to a pneumatic drill. I said to him, "Why don't you see someone about your stutter?"

"Oh, I yu-yu-yu-used to be m-m-m-m-m-much worse than this," he said.

"You are friggin' kidding?" I said.

"N-n-n-n-n-no. D-d-d-d-d-dad h-h-h-had a f-f-f-friend who came to h-h-h-help."

"What did he do to you?"

Still stammering, Ken said, "Well, he came in the house and told me to take down my trousers, I protested, but my father said to do it. I had to lean on the table and part my legs, then he heated up a soldering iron and shoved it up the crack of my backside and I screamed, 'Aaaaaaaarrrggghh!' Then he said, 'Good lad! We'll start on B tomorrow.'" Now I don't know how true this tale is, but the treatment was not a breakthrough in the treatment of speech impedimenta.

Ken worked hard when you could find him, usually at the Cooperage pub, and of course, when Ken was on the phone, the bills doubled. But, as I say, I liked him, he was good company and always smiling. Well, except when his girlfriend turned up.

Cars were starting to fill the garage, and we had to tell people they'd have to wait a couple of days. It felt pretty good. The classier cars were coming in: Rover Vitesse, BMW, Mercedes. Wow, this was cool! Everything was going good. My band, Geordie II, was booked solid and very popular; the company was going great. I'd moved back home with my mother and father. I thought I'd cracked it, and to celebrate we bought a company car, a Jag saloon 420G, huge and daft. There were more things wrong with it than with Italian politics, but it was cheap and posh. People who saw us driving into the garage would say, "Look at them scruffy posh people."

Then came the fateful phone call that changed my life forever. It was February 1980, about three thirty on a cold but sunny ordinary afternoon. "North-East Vinyls," I said into the phone.

"Allo, ees thees Breean Yonson?"

"Close," I said.

"Ah, güt! I am vantink you to come to Lonton to sink viz a groupen."

It was a sexy female voice that I later learned belonged to a woman nicknamed "Olga from the Volga."

"Which group?" I said.

"Zis I cannot tell you. It is a secret."

"Listen to me, darlin'. I've already been bitten by the music factory and I'm still paying for it, so could you be a little more specific?"

"No, I cannot tell. How old are you?"

What the hell was she on about? I said, "I'm thirty-two and probably past a new band's sell-by date."

"Ah," she said. "Ve haf been lookink for you for many days now."

Shit, who was this? What did they want with me? "Listen, lady. I am not driving all the way to London to do an audition with somebody I don't know. Gimme a clue, give me the initials."

"Okay, okay. Zey are ze AC and ze DC."

"You mean AC/DC?"

"Scheiße!" she cried. "I haf said too much!" (By the way, I'm not kiddin'. This is all true.) "You must come," she said.

"I'll think about it. Gimme a ring tomorrow." Holy shit! I've just spent a year building up a nice little earner; I've got money in my pocket, a cute girlfriend, I'm living with my parents, and my band's doing well. Do I throw it all away and get stung by the music business again? AC/DC were a great band and well on their way. Their singer, Bon Scott, had passed away and the boys wanted to carry on. What to do?

The phone rang again thirty minutes later.

"Hey, Brian, remember me? André Jacquemin?"

I said, "André, of course I do. Bond Bug three-wheeler, right?"

"That's right," he said. "Anyway, Brian, I have my own studio and I do a lot of commercials for the telly. I'd like you to do one for me."

Wow! Nobody's asked me to do that before. "It's a Hoover ad, and I'll pay you, plus residuals." Holy shit! That was big money. And then the magic words: "I'll pay for your gas." My mind started buzzing. Maybe I could do the ad, then pop over to audition with AC/DC. "I'll do it," I said.

"See you next Thursday, and don't be late," he said. André was a good man; he did all the Monty Python music and songs, so I knew this was a proper gig.

Simon Robinson was a guy who did rust-proofing not far from our garage. I told him I was going to drive to London to do this gig.

"Not in that Jag, you're not. You'll never make it."

Oh bollocks, he's probably right.

"Tell you what, I've got a Toyota Crown, nearly new. Why don't you take that and we can trade off the cost when I need you?"

"Done!" I said.

Off I went to London Town in my nearly new Toyota. Fifty miles outta Newcastle, and bang—a puncture in the front-left tire. You wouldn't believe it! I changed the wheel and set off again. At Redwood Studios, I heard the music, and it was a little embarrassing. "The new high-powered mover from Hoover. What a beautiful mover!" It was riveting stuff.

I finished the ad by about three thirty P.M. and then I had to go to Vanilla Studio, about three miles away, for AC/DC. Opposite was a café, an old-fashioned one with mince pies and tea and a toothless miserable old hag behind the counter, speaking a language all of her own: "Wotcha, lav. Dat's free paand twenny-free." I sat and ate my mince and onion pie. The top crust seemed strangely welded to the sides of the dish, and no amount of softening would remove it, so I couldn't get to my mince or my onions. "I know," I thought, "I'll go in through the bottom."

"Oi yew, wos gawin' on over dare?" I gave up and walked across the road to the studio and to another life.

In the rehearsal room sat the boys of AC/DC, looking quite bored—they'd been auditioning singers for a month. When I walked in, I introduced myself and Malcolm said, "Ah, you're the Newcastle lad," and promptly gave me a bottle of Newcastle Brown Ale. He said, "Well, what do you wanna sing." I told him "Nutbush City Limits" by Tina Turner.

Eyebrows arched, feet shuffled, Mal looked at the band and said, "Does anybody know it?" Sooo . . . great start then. But they did start playing it, and I belted out the words. That's when a special tingly feeling came over me. I looked around and everyone was smiling. Boy, were these guys good, and boy, did I want to be one of them.

They asked me to stay in London overnight for more rehearsals, but I told them I couldn't, because I had to open my shop in the morning in Newcastle. That kind of stunned them a bit.

I returned home, and the next day I thought it was all a dream. Until the phone rang at one thirty P.M. The rest is history.

The End

THE END

The trouble with "The End" is I don't know where to start. Well, there you have it. My head's starting to hurt thinking of cars past and present that have made my life more fun. The characters I've met, from my first days at work and before. What about Stevie Chance, at Parsons, who described fast cars as going "like shit off a shiny shovel" and the braking as "sticking like shit to a blanket"? Great lads.

I've talked about my early years, living on a council estate, the projects. We weren't poor, but the first time I tasted meat was when I bit my tongue. Luck always plays a part in life; good judgment comes with experience. Religion comes and goes, depending on age or thinking about what comes next.

I'm a lucky lad. I've never believed in God as such, but if there has to be one, then let it be the one who looked after me. He's cool. I'm sure he can't be the same one that people pray to in war; he surely can't be the one who tells people to kill anyone or anything in their way; and he can't be the one that some mad-eyed Southern preacher says keeps talking to him. Mine's just mine, inside my car with me.

Ah! I get it. So that's what that fella Jesus was talking about.